SCIENCE OF AQUACULTURE

SCIENCE OF AQUACULTURE

By

Dr. Arvind N. Shukla

School of Studies of Zoology & Biotechnology

Vikram University

Ujjain (India)

DISCOVERY PUBLISHING HOUSE PVT. LTD.

NEW DELHI-110 002

Published by:

Tilak Wasan

DISCOVERY PUBLISHING HOUSE PVT. LTD.
4383/4B, Ansari Road, Darya Ganj
New Delhi-110 002 (India)
Phone : +91-11-23279245, 43596064-65
Fax : +91-11-23253475
E-mail : parul.wasan@gmail.com
discoverypublishinghouse@gmail.com
web : www.discoverypublishinggroup.com

***First Edition:* 2013**

ISBN: 978-93-5056-296-3

Science of Aquaculture

Printed at:
Dynamic Printers
Delhi

Preface

Aquaculture, also known as aquafarming, is the farming of aquatic organisms such as fish, crustaceans, molluscs and aquatic plants. Aquaculture involves cultivating freshwater and saltwater populations under controlled conditions, and can be contrasted with commercial fishing, which is the harvesting of wild fish. Mariculture refers to aquaculture practised in marine environments.

The output, as reported, from aquaculture would supply one half of the fish and shellfish that is directly consumed by humans. However, there are issues about the reliability of the reported figures. Further, in current aquaculture practice, products from several pounds of wild fish are used to produce one pound of a piscivorous fish like salmon.

Particular kinds of aquaculture include fish farming, shrimp farming, oyster farming, algaculture (such as seaweed farming), and the cultivation of ornamental fish. Particular methods include aquaponics, which integrates fish farming and plant farming.

The indigenous Gunditjmara people in Victoria, Australia may have raised eels as early as 6000 BC. There is evidence that they developed about 100 square kilometres (39 sq mi) of volcanic floodplains in the vicinity of Lake Condah into a complex of channels and dams, that they used woven traps to capture eels, and that capturing and smoking eels supported them year round.

Aquaculture was operating in China circa 2500 BC. When the waters subsided after river floods, some fishes, mainly carp, were trapped in lakes. Early aquaculturists fed their brood using nymphs and silkworm feces, and ate them. A fortunate genetic mutation of carp led to the emergence of goldfish during the Tang Dynasty.

Japanese cultivated seaweed by providing bamboo poles and, later, nets and oyster shells to serve as anchoring surfaces for spores.

In central Europe, early Christian monasteries adopted Roman aquacultural practices. Aquaculture spread in Europe during the Middle Ages, since away from the seacoasts and the big rivers, fish were scarce/expensive. Improvements in transportation during the 19th century made fish easily available and inexpensive, even in inland areas, making aquaculture less popular.

There are two kinds of aquaculture: extensive aquaculture based on local photosynthetical production and intensive aquaculture, in which the fish are fed with external food supply. The management of these two kinds of aquaculture systems are completely different.

Fish farming is the principal form of aquaculture, while other methods may fall under mariculture. Fish farming involves raising fish commercially in tanks or enclosures, usually for food. A facility that releases young (juvenile) fish into the wild for recreational fishing or to supplement a species' natural numbers is generally referred to as a fish hatchery. The most common fish species raised by fish farms are salmon, carp, tilapia, European seabass, catfish and cod.

Aquaculture can be more environmentally damaging than exploiting wild fisheries on a local area basis but has considerably less impact on the global environment on a per kg of production basis. Local concerns include waste handling, side-effects of antibiotics, competition between farmed and wild animals, and using other fish to feed more marketable carnivorous fish. However, research and commercial feed improvements during the 1990s & 2000s have lessened many of these.

Fish waste is organic and composed of nutrients necessary in all components of aquatic food webs. In-ocean aquaculture often produces much higher than normal fish waste concentrations. The waste collects on the ocean bottom, damaging or eliminating bottom-dwelling life. Waste can also decrease dissolved oxygen levels in the water column, putting further pressure on wild animals.

—Author

Contents

CHAPTER

1

Introduction

Aquaculture, also known as aquafarming, is the farming of aquatic organisms such as fish, crustaceans, molluscs and aquatic plants. Aquaculture involves cultivating freshwater and saltwater populations under controlled conditions, and can be contrasted with commercial fishing, which is the harvesting of wild fish. Mariculture refers to aquaculture practised in marine environments.

The output, as reported, from aquaculture would supply one half of the fish and shellfish that is directly consumed by humans. However, there are issues about the reliability of the reported figures. Further, in current aquaculture practice, products from several pounds of wild fish are used to produce one pound of a piscivorous fish like salmon.

Particular kinds of aquaculture include fish farming, shrimp farming, oyster farming, algaculture (such as seaweed farming), and the cultivation of ornamental fish. Particular methods include aquaponics, which integrates fish farming and plant farming.

The indigenous Gunditjmara people in Victoria, Australia may have raised eels as early as 6000 BC. There is evidence that they developed about 100 square kilometres (39 sq mi) of volcanic floodplains in the vicinity of Lake Condah into a complex of channels and dams, that they used woven traps to capture eels, and that capturing and smoking eels supported them year round.

Aquaculture was operating in China circa 2500 BC. When the waters subsided after river floods, some fishes, mainly carp, were trapped in lakes. Early aquaculturists fed their brood using nymphs and silkworm feces, and ate them. A fortunate genetic mutation of carp led to the emergence of goldfish during the Tang Dynasty.

Japanese cultivated seaweed by providing bamboo poles and, later, nets and oyster shells to serve as anchoring surfaces for spores.

In central Europe, early Christian monasteries adopted Roman aquacultural practices. Aquaculture spread in Europe during the Middle Ages, since away from the seacoasts and the big rivers, fish were scarce/expensive. Improvements in transportation during the 19th century made fish easily available and inexpensive, even in inland areas, making aquaculture less popular.

Hawaiians constructed oceanic fish ponds (see Hawaiian aquaculture). A remarkable example is a fish pond dating from at least 1,000 years ago, at Alekoko. Legend says that it was constructed by the mythical Menehune dwarf people.

In 1859 Stephen Ainsworth of West Bloomfield, New York, began experiments with brook trout. By 1864 Seth Green had established a commercial fish hatching operation at Caledonia Springs, near Rochester, New York. By 1866, with the involvement of Dr. W.W. Fletcher of Concord, Massachusetts, artificial fish hatcheries were under way in both Canada and the United States. When the Dildo Island fish hatchery opened in Newfoundland in 1889, it was the largest and most advanced in the world.

Californians harvested wild kelp and attempted to manage supply circa 1900, later labeling it a wartime resource.

About 430 (97%) of the species cultured as of 2007 were domesticated during the 20th century, of which an estimated 106 came in the decade to 2007. Given the long-term importance of agriculture, it is interesting to note that to date only 0.08 per cent of known land plant species and 0.0002 per cent of known land animal species have been domesticated, compared with 0.17 per cent of known marine plant species and 0.13 per cent of known marine animal species. Domestication typically involves about a decade of scientific research. Domesticating aquatic species involve fewer risks to humans than land animals, which took a large toll in human lives. Most major human diseases originated in domesticated animals. through diseases such as smallpox and diphtheria, that like most infectious diseases, move to humans from animals. No human pathogens of comparable virulence have yet emerged from marine species.

Harvest stagnation in wild fisheries and overexploitation of popular marine species, combined with a growing demand for high quality protein encourages aquaculturists to domesticate other marine species.

In 2004, the total world production of fisheries was 140 million tonnes of which aquaculture contributed 45 million tonnes, about one third. The growth rate of worldwide aquaculture has been sustained and rapid, averaging about 8 percent per annum for over thirty years, while the take from wild fisheries has been essentially flat for the last decade. The aquaculture market reached $86 billion in 2009.

Aquaculture is an especially important economic activity in China. Between 1980 and 1997, the Chinese Bureau of Fisheries reports, aquaculture harvests grew at an annual rate of 16.7 percent, jumping from 1,900,000 tonnes (1,870,000 LT; 2,090,000 ST) to nearly 23,000,000 tonnes (23,000,000 LT; 25,000,000 ST). In 2005, China accounted for 70 per cent of world production. Aquaculture is also currently one of the fastest growing areas of food production in the U.S.

Approximately 90 per cent of all U.S. shrimp consumption is farmed and imported. In the past years salmon aquaculture has become a major export in southern Chile, especially in Puerto Montt, Chile's fastest-growing city.

China overwhelmingly dominates the world in reported aquaculture output. They report a total output which is double that of the rest of the world put together. However, there are issues with the accuracy of China's returns.

In 2001, the fisheries scientists Reg Watson and Daniel Pauly expressed concerns in a letter to *Nature*, that China was over reporting its catch from wild fisheries in the 1990s. They said that made it appear that the global catch since 1988 was increasing annually by 300,000 tonnes, whereas it was really shrinking annually by 350,000 tonnes. Watson and Pauly suggested this may be related to China policies where state entities that monitor the economy are also tasked with increasing output. Also, until recently, the promotion of Chinese officials was based on production increases from their own areas.

China disputes this claim. The official Xinhua News Agency quoted Yang Jian, director general of the Agriculture Ministry's Bureau of Fisheries, as saying that China's figures were "basically correct". However, the FAO accepts there are issues with the reliability of China's statistical returns, and currently treats data from China, including the aquaculture data, apart from the rest of the world.

Mariculture

Mariculture is the term used for the cultivation of marine organisms in seawater, usually in sheltered coastal waters. In particular, the farming of marine fish is an example of mariculture, and so also is the farming of marine crustaceans (such as shrimps), molluscs (such as oysters) and seaweed.

Integrated Multi-trophic Aquaculture

Integrated Multi-Trophic Aquaculture (IMTA) is a practice in which the by-products (wastes) from one species are recycled to become inputs (fertilizers, food) for another. Fed aquaculture (e.g. fish, shrimp) is combined with inorganic extractive (e.g. seaweed) and organic extractive (e.g. shellfish) aquaculture to create balanced systems for environmental sustainability (biomitigation), economic stability (product diversification and risk reduction) and social acceptability (better management practices).

"Multi-Trophic" refers to the incorporation of species from different trophic or nutritional levels in the same system. This is one potential distinction from the age-old practice of aquatic polyculture, which could simply be the co-culture of different fish species from the same trophic level. In this case, these organisms may all share the same biological and chemical processes, with few synergistic benefits, which could potentially lead to significant shifts in the ecosystem. Some traditional polyculture systems may, in fact, incorporate a greater diversity of species, occupying several niches, as extensive cultures (low intensity, low management) within the same pond. The "Integrated" in IMTA refers to the more intensive cultivation of the different species in proximity of each other, connected by nutrient and energy transfer through water.

Ideally, the biological and chemical processes in an IMTA system should balance. This is achieved through the appropriate selection and proportions of different species providing different ecosystem functions. The co-cultured species are typically more than just biofilters; they are harvestable crops of commercial value. A working IMTA system can result in greater total production based on mutual benefits to the co-cultured species and improved ecosystem health, even if the production of individual species is lower than in a monoculture over a short term period.

Sometimes the term "Integrated Aquaculture" is used to describe the integration of monocultures through water transfer. For all intents and purposes however, the terms "IMTA" and "integrated aquaculture" differ only in their degree of descriptiveness. Aquaponics, fractionated aquaculture, IAAS (integrated agriculture-aquaculture systems), IPUAS (integrated peri-urban-aquaculture systems), and IFAS (integrated fisheries-aquaculture systems) are other variations of the IMTA concept.

Fish Farming

The farming of fish is the most common form of aquaculture. It involves raising fish commercially in tanks, ponds, or ocean enclosures, usually for food. A facility that releases juvenile fish into the wild for recreational fishing or to supplement a species' natural numbers is generally referred to as a fish hatchery. Fish species raised by fish farms include salmon, bigeye tuna, carp, tilapia, catfish and cod.

In the Mediterranean, young bluefin tuna are netted at sea and towed slowly towards the shore. They are then interned in offshore pens where they are further grown for the market. In 2009, researchers in Australia managed for the first time to coax tuna (Southern bluefin) to breed in landlocked tanks.

Crustaceans

Commercial shrimp farming began in the 1970s, and production grew steeply thereafter. Global production reached more than 1,600,000 tonnes (1,570,000 LT; 1,760,000 ST) in 2003, representing a value of nearly 9,000 million U.S. dollars. About 75 per cent of farmed shrimp is produced in Asia, in particular in China and Thailand. The other 25 per cent is produced mainly in Latin America, where Brazil is the largest producer. Thailand is the largest exporter.

Shrimp farming has changed from its traditional, small-scale form in Southeast Asia into a global industry. Technological advances have led to ever higher densities per unit area, and broodstock is shipped worldwide. Virtually all farmed shrimp are penaeids (i.e., shrimp of the family *Penaeidae*), and just two species of shrimp, the Pacific white shrimp and the giant tiger prawn, account for about 80 per cent of all farmed shrimp. These industrial monocultures are very susceptible to disease, which has decimated shrimp populations across entire regions. Increasing ecological problems, repeated disease outbreaks, and pressure and criticism from both NGOs and consumer countries led to changes in the industry in the late 1990s and generally stronger regulations. In 1999, governments, industry representatives, and environmental organizations initiated a programme aimed at developing and promoting more sustainable farming practices.

Freshwater prawn farming shares many characteristics with, including many problems with marine shrimp farming. Unique problems are introduced by the developmental life cycle of the main species, the giant river prawn.

The global annual production of freshwater prawns (excluding crayfish and crabs) in 2003 was about 280,000 tonnes of which China produced 180,000 tonnes followed by India and Thailand with 35,000 tonnes each. Additionally, China produced about 370,000 tonnes of Chinese river crab.

Oyster Farming

Abalone farming began in the late 1950s and early 1960s in Japan and China. Since the mid-1990s, this industry has become increasingly successful. Over-fishing and poaching have reduced wild populations to the extent that farmed abalone now supplies most abalone meat.

Echinoderms

Commercially harvested echinoderms include sea cucumbers and sea urchins. In China, sea cucumbers are farmed in artificial ponds as large as 1,000 acres (400 ha).

Microalgae, also referred to as phytoplankton, microphytes, or planktonic algae constitute the majority of cultivated algae.

Macroalgae, commonly known as seaweed, also have many commercial and industrial uses, but due to their size and specific requirements, they are not easily cultivated on a large scale and are most often taken in the wild.

Issues

Aquaculture can be more environmentally damaging than exploiting wild fisheries on a local area basis but has considerably less impact on the global environment on a per kg of production basis. Local concerns include waste handling, side-effects of antibiotics, competition between farmed and wild animals, and using other fish to feed more marketable carnivorous fish. However, research and commercial feed improvements during the 1990s & 2000s have lessened many of these.

Fish waste is organic and composed of nutrients necessary in all components of aquatic food webs. In-ocean aquaculture often produces much higher than normal fish waste concentrations. The waste collects on the ocean bottom, damaging or eliminating bottom-dwelling life. Waste can also decrease dissolved oxygen levels in the water column, putting further pressure on wild animals.

The nutritional value of farm-raised tilapia may be compromised due to the amount of corn included in the feed. Corn contains short chain omega-6 fatty acids that contribute to the buildup of these materials in the fish. "Ratios of long-chain omega-6 to long-chain omega-3, AA to EPA respectively, in tilapia averaged about 11:1, compared to much less than 1:1 (indicating more EPA than AA) in both salmon and trout." The US produced 1.5 million tons of tilapia in 2005, with 2.5 million projected by 2010 . Widespread publicity encouraging fish consumption has led to increases in tilapia consumption by those with lower incomes who are trying to eat a balanced diet. The lower amounts of omega-3 and the higher ratios of omega-6 compounds in farmed tilapia raise questions of the health benefits of consuming this fish.

Adequate diets for salmon and other carnivorous fish can be formulated from protein sources such as soy, although soy-based diets may also change in the balance between omega-6 and omega-3 fatty acids.

Impacts on Wild Fish

Salmon farming currently leads to a high demand for wild forage fish. Fish do not actually produce omega-3 fatty acids, but instead accumulate them from either consuming microalgae that produce these fatty acids, as is the case with forage fish like herring and sardines, or, as is the case with fatty predatory fish, like salmon, by eating prey fish that have accumulated omega-3 fatty acids from microalgae. To satisfy this requirement, more than 50 percent of the world fish oil production is fed to farmed salmon.

In addition, as carnivores, salmon require large nutritional intakes of protein, protein which is often supplied to them in the form of forage fish. Consequently, farmed salmon consume more wild fish than they generate as a final product. To produce one pound of farmed salmon, products from several pounds of wild fish are fed to them. As the salmon farming industry expands, it requires more wild forage fish for feed, at a time when seventy five percent of the worlds monitored fisheries are already near to or have exceeded their maximum sustainable yield. The industrial scale extraction of wild forage fish for salmon farming then impacts the survivability of the wild predator fish who rely on them for food.

Fish can escape from coastal pens, where they can interbreed with their wild counterparts, diluting wild genetic stocks. Escaped fish can become invasive, out competing native species.

Coastal Ecosystems

Aquaculture is becoming a significant threat to coastal ecosystems. About 20 per cent of mangrove forests have been destroyed since 1980, partly due to shrimp farming. An extended cost-benefit analysis of the total economic value of shrimp aquaculture built on mangrove ecosystems found that the external costs were much higher than the external benefits. Over four decades, 269,000 hectares (660,000 acres) of

Indonesian mangroves have been converted to shrimp farms. Most of these farms are abandoned within a decade because of the toxin build-up and nutrient loss.

Salmon farms are typically sited in pristine coastal ecosystems which they then pollute. A farm with 200,000 salmon discharges more fecal waste than a city of 60,000 people. This waste is discharged directly into the surrounding aquatic environment, untreated, often containing antibiotics and pesticides." There is also an accumulation of heavy metals on the benthos (seafloor) near the salmon farms, particularly copper and zinc.

Genetic Modification

Salmon have been genetically modified for faster growth, although they are not approved for commercial use, in the face of opposition. One study, in a laboratory setting, found that modified salmon mixed with their wild relatives were aggressive in competing, but ultimately failed.

Prospects

Global wild fisheries are in decline, with valuable habitat such as estuaries in critical condition. The aquaculture or farming of piscivorous fish, like salmon, does not help the problem because they need to eat products from other fish, such as fish meal and fish oil. Studies have shown that salmon farming has major negative impacts on wild salmon, as well as the forage fish that need to be caught to feed them. Fish that are higher on the food chain are less efficient sources of food energy.

Apart from fish and shrimp, some aquaculture undertakings, such as seaweed and filter-feeding bivalve mollusks like oysters, clams, mussels and scallops, are relatively benign and even environmentally restorative. Filter-feeders filter pollutants as well as nutrients from the water, improving water quality. Seaweeds extract nutrients such as inorganic nitrogen and phosphorus directly from the water, and filter-feeding mollusks can extract nutrients as they feed on particulates, such as phytoplankton and detritus.

Some profitable aquaculture cooperatives promote sustainable practices. New methods lessen the risk of biological and chemical pollution through minimizing fish stress, fallowing netpens, and applying Integrated Pest Management. Vaccines are being used more and more to reduce antibiotic use for disease control.

Onshore recirculating aquaculture systems, facilities using polyculture techniques, and properly sited facilities (e.g. offshore areas with strong currents) are examples of ways to manage negative environmental effects.

Recirculating aquaculture systems (RAS) recycle water by circulating it through filters to remove fish waste and food and then recirculating it back into the tanks. This saves water and the waste gathered can be used in compost or, in some cases, could even be treated and used on land. While RAS was developed with freshwater fish in mind, scientist associated with the Agricultural Research Service have found a way to rear saltwater fish using RAS in low-salinity waters. Although saltwater fish are raised in off-shore cages or caught with nets in water that typically has a salinity of 35 parts per thousand (ppt), scientists were able to produce healthy pompano, a saltwater fish, in tanks with a salinity of only 5 ppt. Commercializing low-salinity RAS are predicted to have positive environmental and economical effects. Unwanted nutrients from the fish food would not be added to the ocean and the risk of transmitting diseases between wild and farm-raised fish would greatly be reduced. The price of expensive saltwater fish, such as the pompano and combia used in the experiments, would be reduced. However, before any of this can be done researchers must study every aspect of the fish's lifecycle, including the amount of ammonia and nitrate the fish will tolerate in the water, what to feed the fish during each stage of its lifecycle, the stocking rate that will produce the healthiest fish, etc.

CHAPTER 2

Fish Farming

Fish farming is the principal form of aquaculture, while other methods may fall under mariculture. Fish farming involves raising fish commercially in tanks or enclosures, usually for food. A facility that releases young (juvenile) fish into the wild for recreational fishing or to supplement a species' natural numbers is generally referred to as a fish hatchery. The most common fish species raised by fish farms are salmon, carp, tilapia, European seabass, catfish and cod.

There is an increasing demand for fish and fish protein, which has resulted in widespread overfishing in wild fisheries. Fish farming offers fish marketers another source. However, farming carnivorous fish, such as salmon, does not necessarily reduce pressure on wild fisheries, since carnivorous farmed fish are usually feed fishmeal and fish oil extracted from wild forage fish. In this way, the salmon can consume in weight more wild fish that they weigh themselves. The global returns for fish farming recorded by the FAO in 2008 totalled 33.8 million tonnes worth about $US 60 billion.

There are two kinds of aquaculture: extensive aquaculture based on local photosynthetical production and intensive aquaculture, in which the fish are fed with external food supply. The management of these two kinds of aquaculture systems are completely different.

Extensive Aquaculture

Aqua-Boy, a Norwegian live fish carrier used to service the Marine Harvest fish farms on the West coast of Scotland.

Limiting for growth here is the available food supply by natural sources, commonly zooplankton feeding on pelagic algae or benthic animals, such as crustaceans and mollusks. Tilapia species filter feed directly on phytoplankton, which makes higher production possible. The photosynthetic production can be increased by fertilizing the pond water with artificial fertilizer mixtures, such as potash, phosphorus, nitrogen and micro-elements. Because most fish are carnivorous, they occupy a higher place in the trophic chain and therefore only a tiny fraction of primary photosynthetic production (typically 1%) will be converted into harvest-able fish. As a result, without additional feeding the fish harvest will not exceed 200 kilograms of fish per hectare per year, equivalent to 1 per cent of the gross photosynthetic production.

A second point of concern is the risk of algal blooms. When temperatures, nutrient supply and available sunlight are optimal for algal growth, algae multiply their biomass at an exponential rate, eventually leading to an exhaustion of available nutrients and a subsequent die-off. The decaying algal biomass will deplete the oxygen in the pond water because it blocks out the sun and pollutes it with organic and inorganic solutes (such as ammonium ions), which can (and frequently do) lead to massive loss of fish.

Another option is to use a wetland system such as that of Veta La Palma.

In order to tap all available food sources in the pond, the aquaculturist will choose fish species which occupy different places in the pond ecosystem, e.g., a filter algae feeder such as tilapia, a benthic feeder such as carp or catfish and a zooplankton feeder (various carps) or submerged weeds feeder such as grass carp.

Despite these limitations significant fish farming industries use these methods. In the Czech Republic thousands of natural and semi-natural ponds are harvested each year for trout and carp. The large ponds around Trebon were built from around 1650 and are still in use.

Intensive Aquaculture

In these kinds of systems fish production per unit of surface can be increased at will, as long as sufficient oxygen, fresh water and food are provided. Because of the requirement of sufficient fresh water, a massive water purification system must be integrated in the fish farm. A clever way to achieve this is the combination of hydroponic horticulture and water treatment, see below. The exception to this rule are cages which are placed in a river or sea, which supplements the fish crop with sufficient oxygenated water. Some environmentalists object to this practice.

The cost of inputs per unit of fish weight is higher than in extensive farming, especially because of the high cost of fish feed, which must contain a much higher level of protein (up to 60%) than cattle food and a balanced amino acid composition as well. However, these higher protein level requirements are a consequence of the higher food conversion efficiency (FCR—kg of feed per kg of animal produced) of aquatic animals. Fish like salmon have FCR's in the range of 1.1 kg of feed per kg of salmon whereas chickens are in the 2.5 kg of feed per kg of chicken range. Fish don't have to stand up or keep warm and this eliminates a lot of carbohydrates and fats in the diet, required to provide this energy. This frequently is offset by the lower land costs and the higher productions which can be obtained due to the high level of input control.

Essential here is aeration of the water, as fish need a sufficient oxygen level for growth. This is achieved by bubbling, cascade flow or aqueous oxygen. Catfish, *Clarias* sp. can breathe atmospheric air and can tolerate much higher levels of pollutants than trout or salmon, which makes aeration and water purification less necessary and makes *Clarias* species especially suited for intensive fish production. In some *Clarias* farms about 10 per cent of the water volume can consist of fish biomass.

The risk of infections by parasites like fish lice, fungi (*Saprolegnia* sp.), intestinal worms (such as nematodes or trematodes), bacteria (e.g., *Yersinia* sp, *Pseudomonas* sp.), and protozoa (such as Dinoflagellates) is similar to animal husbandry, especially at high population densities. However, animal husbandry is a larger and more technologically mature area of human agriculture and better solutions to pathogen problem exist. Intensive aquaculture does have to provide adequate water quality (oxygen, ammonia, nitrite, etc.) levels to minimize stress, which makes the pathogen problem more difficult. This means, intensive aquaculture requires tight monitoring and a high level of expertise of the fish farmer.

Very high intensity recycle aquaculture systems (RAS), where there is control over all the production parameters, are being used for high value species. By recycling the water, very little water is used per unit of production. However, the process does have high capital and operating costs. The higher cost structures mean that RAS is only economical for high value products like broodstock for egg production, fingerlings for net pen aquaculture operations, sturgeon production, research animals and some special niche markets like live fish.

Raising ornamental cold water fish (goldfish or koi), although theoretically much more profitable due to the higher income per weight of fish produced, has never been successfully carried out until very recently. The increased incidences of dangerous viral diseases of koi carp, together with the high value of the fish has led to initiatives in closed system koi breeding and growing in a number of countries. Today there are a few commercially successful intensive koi growing facilities in the U.K., Germany and Israel.

Some producers have adapted their intensive systems in an effort to provide consumers with fish that do not carry dormant forms of viruses and diseases.

Integrated Recycling Systems

One of the largest problems with freshwater aquaculture is that it can use a million gallons of water per acre (about 1 m^3 of water per m^2) each year. Extended water purification systems allow for the reuse (recycling) of local water.

The largest-scale pure fish farms use a system derived (admittedly much refined) from the New Alchemy Institute in the 1970s. Basically, large plastic fish tanks are placed in a greenhouse. A hydroponic bed is placed near, above or between them. When tilapia are raised in the tanks, they are able to eat algae, which naturally grows in the tanks when the tanks are properly fertilized.

The tank water is slowly circulated to the hydroponic beds where the tilapia waste feeds commercial plant crops. Carefully cultured microorganisms in the hydroponic bed convert ammonia to nitrates, and the plants are fertilized by the nitrates and phosphates. Other wastes are strained out by the hydroponic media, which doubles as an aerated pebble-bed filter.

This system, properly tuned, produces more edible protein per unit area than any other. A wide variety of plants can grow well in the hydroponic beds. Most growers concentrate on herbs (e.g. parsley and basil), which command premium prices in small quantities all year long. The most common customers are restaurant wholesalers.

Since the system lives in a greenhouse, it adapts to almost all temperate climates, and may also adapt to tropical climates. The main environmental impact is discharge of water that must be salted to maintain the fishes' electrolyte balance.

Current growers use a variety of proprietary tricks to keep fish healthy, reducing their expenses for salt and waste water discharge permits. Some veterinary authorities speculate that ultraviolet ozone disinfectant systems (widely used for ornamental fish) may play a prominent part in keeping the Tilapia healthy with recirculated water.

Irrigation Ditch or Pond Systems

These use irrigation ditches or farm ponds to raise fish. The basic requirement is to have a ditch or pond that retains water, possibly with an above-ground irrigation system (many irrigation systems use buried pipes with headers.) Using this method, one can store one's water allotment in ponds or ditches, usually lined with bentonite clay. In small systems the fish are often fed commercial fish food, and their waste products can help fertilize the fields. In larger ponds, the pond grows water plants and algae as fish food. Some of the most successful ponds grow introduced strains of plants, as well as introduced strains of fish.

Control of water quality is crucial. Fertilizing, clarifying and pH control of the water can increase yields substantially, as long as eutrophication is prevented and oxygen levels stay high. Yields can be low if the fish grow ill from electrolyte stress.

Composite Fish Culture

The composite fish culture system is a technology developed in India by the Indian Council of Agricultural Research in the 1970s. In this system both local and imported fish species, a combination of five or six fish species is used in a single fish pond. These species are selected so that they do not compete for food among them having different types of food habitats. As a result the food available in all the parts of the pond is used. Fish used in this system include catla and silver carp which are surface feeders, rohu a column feeder and mrigal and common carp which are bottom feeders. Other fish will also feed on the excreta of the common carp and this helps contribute to the efficiency of the system which in optimal conditions will produce 3000–6000 kg of fish per hectare per year.

Cage System

Fish cages are placed in lakes, bayous, ponds, rivers or oceans to contain and protect fish until they can be harvested. They can be constructed of a wide variety of components. Fish are stocked in cages, artificially fed, and harvested when they reach market size. A few advantages of fish farming with cages are that many types of waters can be used (rivers, lakes, filled quarries, etc.), many types of fish can be raised, and fish farming can co-exist with sport fishing and other water uses. Cage farming of fishes in open seas is also gaining popularity. Concerns of disease, poaching, poor water quality, etc., lead some to believe that in general, pond systems are easier to manage and simpler to start. Also, past occurrences of cage-failures leading to escapes, have raised concern regarding the culture of non-native fish species in open-water cages. Even though the cage-industry has made numerous technological advances in cage construction in recent years, the concern for escapes remains valid.

Classic Fry Farming

Trout and other sport fish are often raised from eggs to fry or fingerlings and then trucked to streams and released. Normally, the fry are raised in long, shallow concrete tanks, fed with fresh stream water. The fry receive commercial fish food in pellets. While not as efficient as the New Alchemists' method, it is also far simpler, and has been used for many years to stock streams with sport fish. European eel (*Anguilla anguilla*) aquaculturalists procure a limited supply of glass eels, juvenile stages of the European eel which swim north from the Sargasso Sea breeding grounds, for their farms. The European eel is threatened with extinction because of the excessive catch of glass eels by Spanish fishermen and overfishing of adult eels As per 2005, no one has managed to breed the European eel in captivity.

Issues

The issue of feeds in fish farming has been a controversial one. Many cultured fishes (tilapia, carp, catfish, many others) require no meat or fish products in their diets. Top-level carnivores (most salmon species) depend on fish feed of which a portion is usually derived from wild caught fish (anchovies, menhaden, etc.). Vegetable-derived proteins have successfully replaced fish meal in feeds for carnivorous fishes, but vegetable-derived oils have not successfully been incorporated into the diets of carnivores.

Secondly, farmed fish are kept in concentrations never seen in the wild ([e.g. 50,000 fish in a 2-acre (8,100 m^2)] area. with each fish occupying less room than the average bathtub. This can cause several forms of pollution. Packed tightly, fish rub against each other and the sides of their cages, damaging their fins and tails and becoming sickened with various diseases and infections. This also causes stress.

However, fish tend also to be animals that aggregate into large schools at high density. Most successful aquaculture species are schooling species, which do not have social problems at high density. Aquaculturists tend to feel that operating a rearing system above its design capacity or above the social density limit of the fish will result in decreased growth rate and increased FCR (food conversion ratio - kg dry feed/kg of fish produced), which will result in increased cost and risk of health problems along with a decrease in profits. Stressing the animals is not desirable, but the concept of and measurement of stress must be viewed from the perspective of the animal using the scientific method. *Caligus* species, including *Caligus clemensi* and *Caligus rogercresseyi*, can cause deadly infestations of both farm-grown and wild salmon Sea lice are ectoparasites which feed on mucous, blood, and skin, and migrate and latch onto the skin of wild salmon during free-swimming, planktonic *nauplii* and *copepodid* larval stages, which can persist for several days. Large numbers of highly populated, open-net salmon farms can create exceptionally large concentrations of sea lice; when exposed in river estuaries containing large numbers of open-net farms, many young wild salmon are infected, and do not survive as a result. Adult salmon may survive otherwise critical numbers of sea lice, but small, thin-skinned juvenile salmon migrating to sea are highly vulnerable. On the Pacific coast of Canada, the louse-induced mortality of pink salmon in some regions is commonly over 80 per cent.

A 2008 meta-analysis of available data shows that salmon farming reduces the survival of associated wild salmon populations. This relationship has been shown to hold for Atlantic, steelhead, pink, chum, and coho salmon. The decrease in survival or abundance often exceeds 50 per cent.

Diseases and parasites are the most commonly cited reasons for such decreases. Some species of sea lice have been noted to target farmed coho and Atlantic salmon. Such parasites have been shown to have an effect on nearby wild fish. One place that has garnered international media attention is British Columbia's Broughton Archipelago. There, juvenile wild salmon must "run a gauntlet" of large fish farms located off-shore near river outlets before making their way to sea. It is alleged that the farms cause such severe sea lice infestations that one study predicted a 99 per cent collapse in the wild salmon population in another four years. This claim, however, has been criticized by numerous scientists who question the correlation between increased fish farming and increases in sea lice infestation among wild salmon.

Because of parasite problems, some aquaculture operators frequently use strong antibiotic drugs to keep the fish alive (but many fish still die prematurely at rates of up to 30%). In some cases, these drugs have entered the environment. Additionally, the residual presence of these drugs in human food products has become controversial. Use of antibiotics in food production is thought to increase the prevalence of antibiotic resistance in human diseases. At some facilities, the use of antibiotic drugs in aquaculture has decreased considerably due to vaccinations and other techniques. However, most fish farming operations still use antibiotics, many of which escape into the surrounding environment.

The lice and pathogen problems of the 1990s facilitated the development of current treatment methods for sea lice and pathogens. These developments reduced the stress from parasite/pathogen problems. However, being in an ocean environment, the transfer of disease organisms from the wild fish to the aquaculture fish is an ever-present risk.

The very large number of fish kept long-term in a single location contributes to habitat destruction of the nearby areas. The high concentrations of fish produce a significant amount of condensed faeces, often contaminated with drugs, which again affect local waterways. However, these effects are very local to the actual fish farm site and are minimal to non-measurable in high current sites.

Concern remains that resultant bacterial and algae growth strips the water of oxygen, reducing or killing off the local marine life. Once an area has been so contaminated, the fish farms are moved to new, uncontaminated areas. This practice has angered nearby fishermen.

Other potential problems faced by aquaculturists are the obtaining of various permits and water-use rights, profitability, concerns about invasive species and genetic engineering depending on what species are involved, and interaction with the United Nations Convention on the Law of the Sea.

In regards to genetically modified farmed salmon, concern has been raised over their proven reproductive advantage and how it could potentially decimate local fish populations, if released into the wild. Biologist Rick Howard did a controlled laboratory study where wild fish and GMO fish were allowed to breed. The GMO fish crowded out the wild fish in spawning beds, but the offspring were less likely to survive. The Center for Food Safety criticized the FDA's analysis as misguided and dangerous. Federal tests were "insufficient in determining the long-term, unforeseen consequences" of genetic engineering, said Wenonah Hauter, director of Food & Water Watch. The FDA's tests (historically used to determine if a non-GM food was safe) were created before GM products became a reality and are insufficient in determining the long-term, unforeseen consequences of the GM salmon in question. These dated tests cannot determine the salmon's full allergenicity and toxicity. The FDA is reviewing data submitted by AquaBounty, the company that spliced a growth hormone gene into Atlantic salmon, forcing it to grow up to five times faster, and reach market size in about 18 months instead of 3 years. According to the evidence, their salmon might have higher levels of a cancer promoting hormone IGF-1, more antibiotics, and more of a potentially life-threatening allergen(s).

Labelling

In 2005, Alaska passed legislation requiring that any genetically altered fish sold in the state be labeled. In 2006, a Consumer Reports investigation revealed that farm-raised salmon is frequently sold as wild.

In 2008, the US National Organic Standards Board allowed farmed fish to be labeled as organic provided less than 25 per cent of their feed came from wild fish. This decision was criticized by the advocacy group Food & Water Watch as "bending the rules" about organic labeling. In the European Union, fish labeling as to species, method of production and origin, has been required since 2002.

Concerns continue over the labelling of salmon as farmed or wild caught, as well as about the humane treatment of farmed fish. The Marine Stewardship Council has established an Eco label to distinguish between farmed and wild caught salmon, while the RSPCA has established the Freedom Food label to indicate humane treatment of farmed salmon as well as other food products.

Indoor Fish Farming

An alternative to outdoor open ocean cage aquaculture, one in which the risk of environmental damage is high, is through the use of a recirculation aquaculture system (RAS). A RAS is a series of culture tanks and filters where water is continuously recycled and monitored to keep optimal conditions year round. To prevent the deterioration of water quality, the water is treated mechanically through the removal of particulate matter and biologically through the conversion of harmful accumulated chemicals into nontoxic ones.

Other treatments such as UV sterilization, ozonation, and oxygen injection are also used to maintain optimal water quality. Through this system, many of the environmental drawbacks of aquaculture are minimized including escaped fish, water usage, and the introduction of pollutants. The practices also increased feed-use efficiency growth by providing optimum water quality.

One of the drawbacks to recirculation aquaculture systems is water exchange. However, the rate of water exchange can be reduced through aquaponics, such as the incorporation of hydroponically grown plants and denitrification. Both methods reduce the amount of nitrate in the water, and can potentially eliminate the need for water exchanges, closing the aquaculture system from the environment. The amount of interaction between the aquaculture system and the environment can be measured through the cumulative feed burden (CFB kg/M^3), which measures the amount of feed that goes into the RAS relative to the amount of water and waste discharged.

Because of its high capital and operating costs, RAS has generally been restricted to practices such as broodstock maturation, larval rearing, fingerling production, research animal production, SPF (specific pathogen free) animal production, and caviar and ornamental fish production. Although the use of RAS for other species is considered by many aquaculturalists to be impractical, there has been some limited successful implementation of this with high value product such as barramundi, sturgeon and live tilapia in the U.S.

Tanks saturated with carbon dioxide have been used to make fish unconscious. Then their gills are cut with a knife so that the fish bleed out before they are further processed. This is no longer considered a humane method of slaughter. Methods that induce much less physiological stress are electrical or percussive stunning and this has led to the phasing out of the carbon dioxide slaughter method in Europe.

CHAPTER

3

Shrimp Farm

A shrimp farm is an aquaculture business for the cultivation of marine shrimp or prawns for human consumption. Commercial shrimp farming began in the 1970s, and production grew steeply, particularly to match the market demands of the United States, Japan and Western Europe. The total global production of farmed shrimp reached more than 1.6 million tonnes in 2003, representing a value of nearly 9 billion U.S. dollars. About 75 per cent of farmed shrimp is produced in Asia, in particular in China and Thailand. The other 25 per cent is produced mainly in Latin America, where Brazil is the largest producer. The largest exporting nation is Thailand.

Shrimp farming has changed from traditional, small-scale businesses in Southeast Asia into a global industry. Technological advances have led to growing shrimp at ever higher densities, and broodstock is shipped worldwide. Virtually all farmed shrimp are of the family Penaeidae, and just two species – *Penaeus vannamei* (Pacific white shrimp) and *Penaeus monodon* (giant tiger prawn) – account for roughly 80 per cent of all farmed shrimp. These industrial monocultures are very susceptible to diseases, which have caused several regional wipe-outs of farm shrimp populations. Increasing ecological problems, repeated disease outbreaks, and pressure and criticism from both NGOs and consumer countries led to changes in the industry in the late 1990s and generally stronger regulation by governments. In 1999, a programme aimed at developing and promoting more sustainable farming practices was initiated, including governmental bodies, industry representatives, and environmental organizations.

Indonesians and others have farmed shrimp for centuries, using traditional low-density methods. Indonesian brackish water ponds, called *tambaks*, can be traced back as far as the 15th century. They used small scale ponds for monoculture or polycultured with other species, such as milkfish, or in rotation with rice, using the rice paddies for shrimp cultures during the dry season, when no rice could be grown. Such cultures often were in coastal areas or on river banks. Mangrove areas were favored because of their abundant natural shrimp. Wild juvenile shrimp were trapped in ponds and reared on naturally occurring organisms in the water until they reached the desired size for harvesting.

Industrial shrimp farming can be traced to the 1930s, when Japanese agrarians spawned and cultivated Kuruma shrimp (*Penaeus japonicus*) for the first time. By the 1960s, a small industry had developed in Japan. Commercial shrimp farming began to grow rapidly in the late 1960s and early 1970s. Technological advances led to more intensive forms of farming, and growing market demand led to worldwide proliferation of shrimp farms, concentrated in tropical and subtropical regions. Growing consumer demand in the early 1980s coincided with faltering wild catches, creating a booming industry. Taiwan was an early adopter and a major producer in the 1980s; its production collapsed beginning in 1988 due to poor management practices and disease. In Thailand, large-scale production expanded rapidly from 1985. In South America, Ecuador pioneered shrimp farming, where it expanded dramatically from 1978. Brazil had been active in shrimp farming since 1974, but trade boomed there only in the 1990s, making the country a major producer within a few years. Today, there are marine shrimp farms in over fifty countries.

When shrimp farming emerged to satisfy demand that had surpassed the wild fisheries' capacity, the subsistence farming methods of old were rapidly replaced by the more productive practices required to serve a global market. Industrial farming at first followed traditional methods, with so-called "extensive" farms, compensating for low density with increased pond sizes; instead of ponds of just a few hectares, ponds of sizes up to 100 hectares (1.0 km^2) were used and huge areas of mangroves were cleared in some areas. Technological advances made more intensive practices possible that increase yield per area, helping reduce pressure to convert more land. Semi-intensive and intensive farms appeared, where the shrimp were reared on artificial feeds and ponds were actively managed. Although many extensive farms remain, new farms typically are of the semi-intensive kind.

Until the mid-1980s, most farms were stocked with young wild animals, called 'postlarvae', typically caught locally. Postlarvae fishing became an important economic sector in many countries. To counteract the depletion of fishing grounds and to ensure a steady supply of young shrimp, the industry started breeding shrimp in hatcheries.

Shrimp mature and breed only in a marine habitat. The females lay 50,000 to 1 million eggs, which hatch after some 24 hours into tiny nauplii. These nauplii feed on yolk reserves within their bodies, and then metamorphose into zoeae. Shrimp in this second larval stage feed in the wild on algae, and after a few days, morph again into myses. The myses look akin to tiny shrimp, and feed on algae and zooplankton. After another three to four days, they metamorphose a final time into postlarvae: young shrimp that have adult characteristics. The whole process takes about 12 days from hatching. In the wild, postlarvae then migrate into estuaries, which are rich in nutrients and low in salinity. They migrate back into open waters when they mature. Adult shrimp are benthic animals living primarily on the sea bottom.

Supply Chain

In shrimp farming, this lifecycle occurs under controlled conditions. The reasons to do so include more intensive farming, improved size control resulting in more uniformly sized shrimp, and better predator control, but also the ability to accelerate growth and maturation by controlling the climate (especially in farms in the temperate zones, using greenhouses). There are three different stages:

- *Hatcheries* breed shrimp and produce nauplii or even postlarvae, which they sell to farms. Large shrimp farms maintain their own hatcheries and sell nauplii or postlarvae to smaller farms in the region.
- *Nurseries* grow postlarvae and accustom them to the marine conditions in the growout ponds.
- In the *growout* ponds the shrimp are grown from juveniles to marketable size, which takes between three to six months.

Most farms produce one to two harvests a year; in tropical climates, even three are possible. Because of the need for salt water, shrimp farms are located on or near a coast. Inland shrimp farms have also been tried in some regions, but the need to ship salt water and competition for land with agricultural users led to problems. Thailand banned inland shrimp farms in 1999.

Small-scale hatcheries are very common throughout Southeast Asia. Often run as family businesses and using a low-technology approach, they use small tanks (less than ten tons) and often low animal densities. They are susceptible to disease, but due to their small size, they can typically restart production quickly after disinfection. The survival rate is anywhere between zero and 90 per cent, depending on a wide range of factors, including disease, the weather, and the experience of the operator.

Greenwater hatcheries are medium-sized hatcheries using large tanks with low animal densities. To feed the shrimp larvae, an algal bloom is induced in the tanks. The survival rate is about 40 per cent.

Galveston hatcheries (named after Galveston, Texas, where they were developed) are large-scale, industrial hatcheries using a closed and tightly controlled environment. They breed the shrimp at high densities in large (15 to 30 ton) tanks. Survival rates vary between zero and 80 per cent, but typically achieve 50 per cent.

In hatcheries, the developing shrimp are fed on a diet of algae and later also brine shrimp nauplii, sometimes (especially in industrial hatcheries) augmented by artificial diets. The diet of later stages also includes fresh or freeze-dried animal protein, for example krill. Nutrition and medication (such as antibiotics) fed to the brine shrimp nauplii are passed on to the shrimp that eat them.

Many farms have nurseries where the postlarval shrimp are grown into juveniles for another three weeks in separate ponds, tanks, or so-called raceways. A raceway is a rectangular, long, shallow tank through which water flows continuously.

In a typical nursery, there are 150 to 200 animals per square meter. They are fed on a high-protein diet for at most three weeks before they are moved to the growout ponds. At that time, they weigh between one and two grams. The water salinity is adjusted gradually to that of the growout ponds.

Farmers refer to postlarvae as "PLs", with the number of days suffixed (i.e., PL-1, PL-2, etc.). They are ready to be transferred to the growout ponds after their gills have branched, which occurs around PL-13 to PL-17 (about 25 days after hatching). Nursing is not absolutely necessary, but is favored by many farms because it makes for better food utilization, improves the size uniformity, helps use the infrastructure better, and can be done in a controlled environment to increase the harvest. The main disadvantage of nurseries is that some of the postlarval shrimp die upon the transfer to the growout pond.

Some farms do not use a nursery, but stock the postlarvae directly in the growout ponds after having acclimated them to the appropriate temperature and salinity levels in an acclimation tank. Over the course of a few days, the water in these tanks is changed gradually to match that of the growout ponds. The animal density should not exceed 500/litre for young postlarvae and 50/litre for larger ones, such as PL-15.

In the growout phase, the shrimp are grown to maturity. The postlarvae are transferred to ponds where they are fed until they reach marketable size, which takes about another three to six months. Harvesting the shrimp is done by fishing them from the ponds using nets or by draining the ponds. Pond sizes and the level of technical infrastructure vary.

Extensive shrimp farms using traditional low-density methods are invariably located on a coast and often in mangrove areas. The ponds range from just a few to more than 100 hectares; shrimp are stocked at low densities (2-3 animals per square meter, or 25,000/ha) . The tides provide for some water exchange, and the shrimp feed on naturally occurring organisms. In some areas, farmers even grow wild shrimp by just opening the gates and impounding wild larvae. Prevalent in poorer or less developed countries where land prices are low, extensive farms produce annual yields from 50 to 500 kg/ha of shrimp (head-on weight). They have low production costs (US$1–3/kg live shrimp), are not very labour intensive, and do not require advanced technical skills.

Semi-intensive farms do not rely on tides for water exchange, but use pumps and a planned pond layout. They can therefore be built above the high tide line. Pond sizes range from 2 to 30 ha; the stocking densities range from 10 to

30/square metre (100,000-300,000/ha). At such densities, artificial feeding using industrially prepared shrimp feeds and fertilizing the pond to stimulate the growth of naturally occurring organisms become a necessity. Annual yields range from 500 to 5,000 kg/ha, while production costs are in the range of US$2–6/kg live shrimp. With densities above 15 animals per square metre, aeration is often required to prevent oxygen depletion. Productivity varies depending upon water temperature, thus it is common to have larger sized shrimp in some seasons than in others.

Intensive farms use even smaller ponds (0.1-1.5 ha) and even higher stocking densities. The ponds are actively managed: they are aerated, there is a high water exchange to remove waste products and maintain water quality, and the shrimp are fed on specially designed diets, typically in the form of formulated pellets. Such farms produce annual yields between 5,000 and 20,000 kg/ha; a few super-intensive farms can produce as much as 100,000 kg/ha. They require an advanced technical infrastructure and highly trained professionals for constant monitoring of water quality and other pond conditions; their production costs are in the range of US$4–8/kg live shrimp.

Estimates on the production characteristics of shrimp farms vary. Most studies agree that about 55-60 per cent of all shrimp farms worldwide are extensive farms, another 25-30 per cent are semi-intensive, and the rest are intensive farms. Regional variation is high, though, and reports wide discrepancies in the percentages claimed for individual countries by different studies.

Feeding the Shrimp

While extensive farms mainly rely on the natural productivity of the ponds, more intensively managed farms rely on artificial shrimp feeds, either exclusively or as a supplement to the organisms that naturally occur in a pond. A food chain is established in the ponds, based on the growth of phytoplankton. Fertilizers and mineral conditioners are used to boost the growth of the phytoplankton to accelerate the growth of the shrimp. Waste from the artificial food pellets and shrimp excrement can lead to the eutrophication of the ponds.

Artificial feeds come in the form of specially formulated, granulated pellets that disintegrate quickly. Up to 70 per cent of such pellets are wasted, as they decay before the shrimp have eaten them. They are fed two to five times daily; the feeding can be done manually either from ashore or from boats, or using mechanized feeders distributed all over a pond. The feed conversion rate (FCR), i.e. the amount of food needed to produce a unit (e.g. one kilogram) of shrimp, is claimed by the industry to be around 1.2-2.0 in modern farms, but this is an optimum value that is not always attained in practice. For a farm to be profitable, a feed conversion rate below 2.5 is necessary; in older farms or under suboptimal pond conditions, the ratio may easily rise to 4:1. Lower FCRs result in a higher profit for the farm.

Although there are many species of shrimp and prawn, only a few of the larger ones are actually cultivated, all of which belong to the family of penaeids (family Penaeidae), and within it to the genus *Penaeus*. Many species are unsuitable for farming: they are too small to be profitable, or simply stop growing when crowded together, or are too susceptible to diseases. The two species dominating the market are:

- Pacific white shrimp (*Litopenaeus vannamei*, also called "whiteleg shrimp") is the main species cultivated in western countries. Native to the Pacific coast from Mexico to Peru, it grows to a size of 23 cm. *L. vannamei* accounts for 95 per cent of the production in Latin America. It is easy to breed in captivity, but succumbs to the Taura disease.
- Giant tiger prawn (*P. monodon*, also known as "black tiger shrimp") occurs in the wild in the Indian Ocean and in the Pacific Ocean from Japan to Australia. The largest of all the cultivated shrimp, it can grow to a length of 36 cm

and is farmed in Asia. Because of its susceptibility to whitespot disease and the difficulty of breeding it in captivity, it is gradually being replaced by *L. vannamei* since 2001.

Together, these two species account for about 80 per cent of the whole farmed shrimp production. Other species being bred are:

- Kuruma shrimp in an aquaculture observation tank in Taiwan.
- Western blue shrimp (*P. stylirostris*) was a popular choice for shrimp farming in the western hemisphere, until the IHHN virus wiped out nearly the whole population in the late 1980s. A few stocks survived and became resistant against this virus. When it was discovered that some of these were also resistant against the Taura virus, some farms again bred *P. stylirostris* from 1997 on.
- Chinese white shrimp (*P. chinensis*, also known as the *fleshy prawn*) occurs along the coast of China and the western coast of Korea and is being farmed in China. It grows to a maximum length of only 18 cm, but tolerates colder water (min. 16°C). Once a major factor on the world market, it is today used almost exclusively for the Chinese domestic market after a disease wiped out nearly all the stocks in 1993.
- Kuruma shrimp (*P. japonicus*) is farmed primarily in Japan and Taiwan, but also in Australia; the only market is in Japan, where live Kuruma shrimp reach prices of the order of US$100 per pound ($220/kg).
- Indian white shrimp (*P. indicus*) is a native of the coasts of the Indian Ocean and is widely bred in India, Iran and the Middle East and along the African shores.
- Banana shrimp (*P. merguiensis*) is another cultured species from the coastal waters of the Indian Ocean, from Oman to Indonesia and Australia. It can be grown at high densities.

Several other species of *Penaeus* play only a very minor role in shrimp farming. Some other kinds of shrimp also can be farmed, e.g. the "Akiami paste shrimp" or *Metapenaeus* spp. Their total production from aquaculture is of the order of only about 25,000 tonnes per year, small in comparison to that of the penaeids.

Diseases

There are a variety of lethal viral diseases that affect shrimp. In the densely populated, monocultural farms such virus infections spread rapidly and may wipe out whole shrimp populations. A major transfer vector of many of these viruses is the water itself; and thus any virus outbreak also carries the danger of decimating shrimp living in the wild.

Yellowhead disease, called *Hua leung* in Thai, affects *P. monodon* throughout Southeast Asia. It had been reported first in Thailand in 1990. The disease is highly contagious and leads to mass mortality within 2 to 4 days. The cephalothorax of an infected shrimp turns yellow after a period of unusually high feeding activity ending abruptly, and the then moribund shrimp congregate near the surface of their pond before dying.

Whitespot syndrome is a disease caused by a family of related viruses. First reported in 1993 from Japanese *P. japonicus* cultures, it spread throughout Asia and then to the Americas. It has a wide host range and is highly lethal, leading to mortality rates of 100 per cent within days. Symptoms include white spots on the carapace and a red hepatopancreas. Infected shrimp become lethargic before they die.

Taura syndrome was first reported from shrimp farms on the Taura river in Ecuador in 1992. The host of the virus causing the disease is *P. vannamei*, one of the two most commonly farmed shrimp. The disease spread rapidly, mainly through the shipping of infected animals and broodstock. Originally confined to farms in the Americas, it has also been propagated to Asian shrimp farms with the introduction of *L. vannamei* there. Birds are thought to be a route of infection between farms within one region.

Infectious hypodermal and hematopoietic necrosis (IHHN) is a disease that causes mass mortality among *P. stylirostris* (as high as 90%) and severe deformations in *L. vannamei*. It occurs in Pacific farmed and wild shrimp, but not in wild shrimp on the Atlantic coast of the Americas.

There are also a number of bacterial infections that are lethal to shrimp. The most common is vibriosis, caused by bacteria of the *Vibrio* species. The shrimp become weak and disoriented, and may have dark wounds on the cuticle. The mortality rate can exceed 70 per cent. Another bacterial disease is necrotising hepatopancreatitis (NHP); symptoms include a soft exoskeleton and fouling. Most such bacterial infections are strongly correlated to stressful conditions, such as overcrowded ponds, high temperatures, and poor water quality, factors that positively influence the growth of bacteria. Treatment is done using antibiotics. Importing countries have repeatedly placed import bans on shrimp containing various antibiotics. One such antibiotic is chloramphenicol, which has been banned in the European Union since 1994, but continues to pose problems.

With their high mortality rates, diseases represent a very real danger to shrimp farmers, who may lose their income for the whole year if their ponds are infected. Since most diseases cannot yet be treated effectively, the industry's efforts are focused on preventing disease outbreak in the first place. Active water quality management helps avoid poor pond conditions favorable to the spread of diseases, and instead of using larvae from wild catches, specific pathogen free broodstocks raised in captivity in isolated environments and certified not to carry diseases are used increasingly. To avoid introducing diseases into such disease-free populations on a farm, there is also a trend to create more controlled environments in the ponds of semi-intensive farms, such as by lining them with plastic to avoid soil contact, and by minimizing water exchange in the ponds.

Economy

The total global production of farmed shrimp reached 2.5 million tonnes in 2005. This accounts for 42 per cent of the total shrimp production that year (farming and wild catches combined). The largest single market for shrimp is the United States, importing between 500-600,000 tonnes of shrimp products yearly in the years 2003-2009. About 200,000 tonnes yearly are imported by Japan, while the European Union imported in 2006 another about 500,000 tonnes of tropical shrimps, with the largest importers being Spain and France. The EU also is a major importer of coldwater shrimp from catches, mainly common shrimp *(Crangon crangon)* and *Pandalidae* such as *Pandalus borealis*; in 2006, these imports accounted for about another 200,000 tonnes.

The import prices for shrimp fluctuate wildly. In 2003, the import price per kilogram shrimp in the United States was US$ 8.80, slightly higher than in Japan at US$8.00. The average import price in the EU was only about US$5.00/kg; this much lower value is explained by the fact that the EU imports more coldwater shrimp (from catches) that are much smaller than the farmed warm water species, and thus attain lower prices. In addition, Mediterranean Europe prefers head-on shrimp, which weigh approximately 30 per cent more, but have a lower unit price.

About 75 per cent of the world production of farmed shrimp comes from Asian countries; the two leading nations being China and Thailand, closely followed by Vietnam, Indonesia, and India. The other 25 per cent are produced in the western hemisphere, where Latin American countries (Brazil, Ecuador, Mexico) dominate. In terms of export, Thailand is by far the leading nation, with a market share of more than 30 per cent, followed by China, Indonesia, and India, accounting each for about 10 per cent. Other major export nations are Vietnam, Bangladesh, and Ecuador. Thailand exports nearly all of its production, while China uses most of its shrimp in the domestic market. The only other major export nation that has a strong domestic market for farmed shrimp is Mexico.

Disease problems have repeatedly impacted the shrimp production negatively. Besides the near-wipeout of *P. chinensis* in 1993, there were outbreaks of viral diseases that led to marked declines in the per-country production in 1996/97 in Thailand and repeatedly in Ecuador. In Ecuador alone, production suffered heavily in 1989 (IHHN), 1993 (Taura), and 1999 (whitespot). Another reason for sometimes wild changes in shrimp farm output are the import regulations of the destination countries, which do not allow shrimp contaminated by chemicals or antibiotics to be imported.

In the 1980s and through much of the 1990s, shrimp farming promised high profits. The investments required for extensive farms were low, especially in regions with low land prices and wages. For many tropical countries, especially those with poorer economies, shrimp farming was an attractive business, offering jobs and incomes for poor coastal populations and has, due to the high market prices of shrimp, provided many developing countries with non-negligible foreign currency earnings. Many shrimp farms were funded initially by the World Bank or substantially subsidized by local governments.

In the late 1990s, the economic situation changed. Governments and farmers alike were under increasing pressure from NGOs and the consumer countries, who criticized the practices of the trade. International trade conflicts erupted, such as import bans by consumer countries on shrimp containing antibiotics, the United States' shrimp import ban against Thailand in 2004 as a measure against Thai shrimp *fishers* not using turtle excluder devices in their nets, or the "anti-dumping" case initiated by U.S. shrimp fishers in 2002 against shrimp farmers worldwide, which resulted two years later in the U.S. imposing antidumping tariffs of the order of about 10 per cent against many producer countries (except China, which received a 112% duty). Diseases caused significant economic losses. In Ecuador, where shrimp farming was a major export sector (the other two are bananas and oil), the whitespot outbreak of 1999 caused an estimated 130,000 workers to lose their jobs. Furthermore, shrimp prices dropped sharply in 2000. All of these factors contributed to the slowly growing acceptance by farmers that improved farming practices were needed, and resulted in tighter government regulation of the business, both of which internalized some of the external costs that were ignored during the boom years.

Shrimp farming offers significant employment opportunities, which may help alleviate the poverty of the local coastal populations in many areas, if it is properly managed. The published literature on that topic shows large discrepancies, and much of the available data are of anecdotal nature. Estimates of the labor intensity of shrimp farms range from about one-third to three times more than when the same area was used for rice paddies, with much regional variation and depending on the type of farms surveyed. In general, intensive shrimp farming requires more labor per unit area than extensive farming. Extensive shrimp farms cover much more land area and are often, but not always, located in areas where no agricultural land uses are possible. Supporting industries such as feed production or storage, handling, and trade companies should also not be neglected, even if not all of them are exclusive to shrimp farming.

Typically, workers on a shrimp farm can get better wages than with other employment. A global estimate from one study is that a shrimp farm worker can earn 1.5-3 times as much as in other jobs; a study from India arrived at a salary increase of about 1.6, and a report from Mexico states the lowest paid job at shrimp farms was paid in 1996 at 1.22 times the average worker salary in the country.

NGOs have frequently criticized that most of the profits went to large conglomerates instead of to the local population. While this may be true in certain regions, such as Ecuador, where most shrimp farms are owned by large companies, it does not apply in all cases. For instance in Thailand, most farms are owned by small local entrepreneurs, although there is a trend to vertically integrate the industries related to shrimp farming from feed producers to food processors and trade companies. A 1994 study reported a farmer in Thailand could increase his income by a factor of ten by switching from growing rice to farming shrimp. An Indian study from 2003 arrives at similar figures for shrimp farming in the East Godavari district in Andhra Pradesh.

Whether the local population benefits from shrimp farming is also dependent on the availability of sufficiently trained people. Extensive farms tend to offer mainly seasonal jobs during harvest that do not require much training. In Ecuador, many of these positions are known to have been filled by migrant workers. More intensive farms have a need for year-round labor in more sophisticated jobs.

Marketing

For commercialization, shrimp are graded and marketed in different categories. From complete shrimp (known as "head-on, shell-on" or HOSO) to peeled and deveined (P&D), any presentation is available in stores. The animals are graded by their size uniformity and then also by their count per weight unit, with larger shrimp attaining higher prices.

Ecological Impacts Plants

A toxic sludge oozing out of the bottom of a shrimp pond of a farm in Indonesia after the harvest. The liquid pictured here contained sulfuric acid resulting from oxidation of pyrite contained in the soil. Such contamination of a pond leads to stunted growth of the shrimp and increased mortality rates; the growth of the plankton is reduced drastically. Liming can be applied to counteract to some extent the acidification of the water in ponds on acid sulfate soil, such as mangrove soils.

Shrimp farms of all types, from extensive to super-intensive, can cause severe ecological problems wherever they are located. For extensive farms, huge areas of mangroves were cleared, reducing biodiversity. During the 1980s and 1990s, about 35 per cent of the world's mangrove forests had vanished. Shrimp farming was a major cause of this, accounting for over a third of it according to one study; other studies report between 5 per cent and 10 per cent globally, with enormous regional variability. Other causes of mangrove destruction are population pressure, logging, pollution from other industries, or conversion to other uses such as salt pans. Mangroves, through their roots, help stabilize a coastline and capture sediments; their removal has led to a marked increase of erosion and less protection against floods. Mangrove estuaries are also especially rich and productive ecosystems and provide the spawning grounds for many species of fish, including many commercially important ones. Many countries have protected their mangroves and forbidden the construction of new shrimp farms in tidal or mangrove areas. The enforcement of the respective laws is often problematic, though, and especially in the least developed countries such as Bangladesh, Myanmar, or Vietnam the conversion of mangroves to shrimp farms remains an issue for areas such as the Myanmar Coast mangroves.

Intensive farms, while reducing the direct impact on the mangroves, have other problems. Their nutrient-rich effluents (industrial shrimp feeds disintegrate quickly, as little as 30 per cent are actually eaten by the shrimp with a corresponding economic loss to the farmer, the rest is wasted) are typically discharged into the environment, seriously upsetting the ecological balance. These waste waters contain significant amounts of chemical fertilizers, pesticides, and antibiotics that cause pollution of the environment. Furthermore, releasing antibiotics in such ways injects them into the food chain and increases the risks of bacteria becoming resistant against them. However, most aquatic bacteria, unlike bacteria associated with terrestrial animals, are not zoonotic. Only a few disease transfers from animals to humans have been reported.

Prolonged use of a pond can lead to an incremental buildup of a sludge at the pond's bottom from waste products and excrement. The sludge can be removed mechanically, or dried and plowed to allow biodecomposition, at least in areas without acid problems. Flushing a pond never completely removes this sludge, and eventually, the pond is abandoned, leaving behind a wasteland, with the soil made unusable for any other purposes due to the high levels of salinity, acidity, and toxic chemicals. A typical pond in an extensive farm can be used only a few years. An Indian study estimated the time to rehabilitate such lands to about 30 years. Thailand has banned inland shrimp farms since 1999 because they caused too much destruction of agricultural lands due to salination. A Thai study estimated 60 per cent of the shrimp farming area in Thailand was abandoned in the years 1989-1996. Many of these problems stem from using mangrove land that has high natural pyrite content (acid sulfate soil) and poor drainage. The shift to semi-intensive farming requires higher elevations for drain harvesting and low sulfide (pyrite) content to prevent acid formation when the soils shift from anaerobic to aerobic conditions.

The global nature of the shrimp farming business, and in particular the shipment of broodstock and hatchery products, throughout the world have not only introduced various shrimp species as exotic species, but also distributed the diseases the shrimp may carry worldwide. As a consequence, most broodstock shipments require health certificates and/or to have specific pathogen free (SPF) status. Many organizations lobby actively for consumers to avoid buying farmed shrimp; some also advocate the development of more sustainable farming methods. A joint programme of the World Bank, the Network of Aquaculture Centres in Asia-Pacific (NACA), the WWF, and the FAO was established in August 1999 to study and propose improved practices for shrimp farming. Some existing attempts at sustainable export-oriented shrimp farming marketing the shrimp as "ecologically produced" are criticized by NGOs as being dishonest and trivial window-dressing.

Yet, the industry has been slowly changing since about 1999. It has adopted the "best management practices" developed by the World Bank programme, for example, and others. and instituted educational programmes to promote them. Due to the mangrove protection laws enacted in many countries, new farms are usually of the semi-intensive kind, which are best constructed outside mangrove areas anyway. There is a trend to create even more tightly controlled environments in these farms, with the hope to achieve better disease prevention. Waste water treatment has attracted considerable attention; modern shrimp farms routinely have effluent treatment ponds where sediments are allowed to settle at the bottom and other residuals are filtered. As such improvements are costly, the World Bank programme also recommends low-intensity polyculture farming for some areas. Since it has been discovered that mangrove soils are effective in filtering waste waters and tolerate high nitrate levels, the industry has also developed an interest in mangrove reforestation, although its contributions in that area are still minor. The long-term effects of these recommendations and industry trends cannot be evaluated conclusively yet.

Social Changes

Shrimp farming in many cases has far-reaching effects on the local coastal population. Especially in the boom years of the 1980s and 1990s, when the business was largely unregulated in many countries, the very fast expansion of the industry caused significant changes that sometimes were detrimental to the local population. Conflicts can be traced back to two root causes: competition for common resources such as land and water, and changes induced by wealth redistribution.

A significant problem causing much conflict in some regions, for instance in Bangladesh, are the land use rights. With shrimp farming, a new industry expanded into coastal areas and started to make exclusive use of previously public resources. In some areas, the rapid expansion resulted in the local coastal population being denied access to the coast by a continuous strip of shrimp farms with serious impacts on the local fisheries. Such problems were compounded by poor ecological practices that caused a degradation of common resources (such as excessive use of freshwater to control the salinity of the ponds, causing the water table to sink and leading to the salination of freshwater aquifers by an inflow of salt water). With growing experience, countries usually introduced stronger governmental regulations and have taken steps to mitigate such problems, for instance through land zoning legislations. Some late adopters have even managed to avoid some problems through proactive legislation, e.g. Mexico. The situation in Mexico is unique owing to the strongly government-regulated market. Even after the liberalisation in the early 1990s, most shrimp farms are still owned and controlled by locals or local co-ops (*ejidos*).

Social tensions have occurred due to changes in the wealth distribution within populations. The effects of this are mixed, though, and the problems are not unique to shrimp farming. Changes in the distribution of wealth tend to induce changes in the power structure within a community. In some cases, there is a widening gap between the general population and local élites who have easier access to credits, subsidies, and permits and thus are more likely to become shrimp farmers and benefit more. In Bangladesh, on the other hand, local élites were opposing shrimp farming, which was controlled largely by an urban élite. Land concentrations in a few hands has been recognized to carry an increased risk of social and economic problems developing, especially if the landowners are non-local.

In general, it has been found that shrimp farming is accepted best and introduced most easily and with the greatest benefits for the local communities if the farms are owned by local people instead of by restricted remote élites or large companies because local owners have a direct interest in maintaining the environment and good relations with their neighbors, and because it avoids the formation of large-scale land property.

CHAPTER 4

Oyster Farming

Oyster farming is an aquaculture (or mariculture) practice in which oysters are raised for human consumption. Oyster farming most likely developed in tandem with pearl farming, a similar practice in which oysters are farmed for the purpose of developing pearls. It was practiced by the ancient Romans as early as the 1st century BC on the Italian peninsula and later in Britain for export to Rome. The French oyster industry has relied on aquacultured oysters since the late 18th century.

Oysters naturally grow in estuarine bodies of brackish water. When farmed, the temperature and salinity of the water are controlled (or at least monitored), so as to induce spawning and fertilization, as well as to speed the rate of maturation – which can take several years.

Three methods of cultivation are commonly used. In each case oysters are cultivated to the size of "spat," the point at which they attach themselves to a substrate. The substrate is known as a "culch" or "cultch". The loose spat may be allowed to mature further to form "seed" oysters with small shells. In either case (spat or seed stage), they are then set out to mature. The maturation technique is where the cultivation method choice is made.

In one method the spat or seed oysters are distributed over existing oyster beds and left to mature naturally. Such oysters will then be collected using the methods for fishing wild oysters, such as dredging.

In the second method the spat or seed may be put in racks, bags, or cages (or they may be glued in threes to vertical ropes) which are held above the bottom. Oysters cultivated in this manner may be harvested by lifting the bags or racks to the surface and removing mature oysters, or simply retrieving the larger oysters when the enclosure is exposed at low tide. The latter method may avoid losses to some predators, but is more expensive.

In the third method the spat or seed are placed in a culch within an artificial maturation tank. The maturation tank may be fed with water that has been especially prepared for the purpose of accelerating the growth rate of the oysters. In particular the temperature and salinity of the water may be altered somewhat from nearby ocean water. The carbonate minerals calcite and aragonite in the water may help oysters develop their shells faster and may also be included in the water processing prior to introduction to the tanks. This latter cultivation technique may be the least susceptible to predators and poaching, but is the most expensive to build and to operate. The Pacific oyster *C. gigas* is the species most commonly used with this type of farming.

Oyster predators include starfish, oyster drill snails, stingrays, Florida stone crabs, birds, such as oystercatchers and gulls, as well as humans.

Diseases that can affect either farmed *C. virginica* or *C. gigas* oysters include *Perkinsus marinus* (Dermo) and *Haplosporidium nelsoni* (MSX). However, *C. viginicus* are much more susceptible to Dermo or MSX infections than are the *C. gigas* species of oyster. Pathogens of *O. edulis* oysters include

Marteilia refringens and *Bonamia ostrea*. In the north Atlantic Ocean, oyster crabs may live in an endosymbiotic commensal relationship within a host oyster. Since oyster crabs are considered a food delicacy they may not be removed from young farmed oysters, as they can themselves be harvested for sale.

The word oyster is used as a common name for a number of distinct groups of bivalve molluscs which live in marine or brackish habitats. The valves are highly calcified.

Some kinds of oyster are commonly consumed by humans, cooked or raw. Other kinds, such as pearl oysters, are not.

Almost all shell-bearing molluscs can secrete pearls, yet most are not very valuable.

Pearl oysters are not closely related to true oysters, being members of a distinct family, the *feathered oysters* (Pteriidae). Both cultured pearls and natural pearls can be obtained from pearl oysters, though other molluscs, such as the freshwater mussels, also yield pearls of commercial value.

The largest pearl-bearing oyster is the marine *Pinctada maxima,* which is roughly the size of a dinner plate. Not all individual oysters produce pearls naturally. In fact, in a harvest of three tons of oysters, only three to four oysters produce perfect pearls.

In nature, pearl oysters produce natural pearls by covering a minute invading parasite with nacre, not by ingesting a grain of sand. Over the years, the irritating object is covered with enough layers of nacre to form what is known as a pearl. There are many different types, colours and shapes of pearl; these qualities depend on the natural pigment of the nacre, and the shape of the original irritant.

Pearl farmers can culture a pearl by placing a nucleus, usually a piece of polished mussel shell, inside the oyster. In three to six years, the oyster can produce a perfect pearl. These pearls are not as valuable as natural pearls, but look exactly the same. In fact, since the beginning of the 20th century, when several researchers discovered how to produce artificial pearls, the cultured pearl market has far outgrown the natural pearl market. Natural pearls have become increasingly scarce, and a necklace with only natural pearls can easily cost several hundred thousand U.S. dollars.

Other Types of Oysters

A number of bivalve molluscs (other than edible oysters and pearl oysters) also have common names that include the word "oyster", usually because they either taste or look like oysters, or because they yield noticeable pearls. Examples include:

- Thorny oysters (Spondylidae)
- Pilgrim oysters (a kind of scallop)
- Saddle oysters (*Anomia ephippium*)

Oysters are filter feeders, drawing water in over their gills through the beating of cilia. Suspended plankton and particles are trapped in the mucus of a gill, and from there are transported to the mouth, where they are eaten, digested and expelled as faeces or pseudofaeces. Oysters feed most actively at temperatures above 10°C (50°F). An oyster can filter up to 5 litres (1.3 US gal) of water per hour. Chesapeake Bay's once flourishing oyster population historically filtered excess nutrients from the estuary's entire water volume every three to four days. Today that would take nearly a year. Excess sediment, nutrients, and algae can result in the eutrophication of a body of water. Oyster filtration can mitigate these pollutants.

In addition to their gills, oysters can also exchange gases across their mantle, which is lined with many small, thin-walled blood vessels. A small, three-chambered heart, lying under the adductor muscle, pumps colorless blood to all parts of the body. At the same time, two kidneys, located on the underside of the muscle, remove waste products from the blood.

While some oysters have two sexes (European Oyster & Olympia Oyster), their reproductive organs contain both eggs and sperm. Because of this, it is technically possible for an oyster to fertilize its own egg. The gonads surround the digestive organs, and are made up of sex cells, branching tubules and connective tissue.

Once the female is fertilized, they discharge millions of eggs into the water. The larvae develop in about six hours and swim around for about two to three weeks. After that, they settle on a bed and mature within a year.

A group of oysters is commonly called a bed or oyster reef.

The largest oyster-producing body of water is located in Chesapeake Bay, although these beds are starting to lower in numbers due to overfishing and pollution. Large beds of edible oysters are also found in Japan and Australia.

As a keystone species, oysters provide habitat for many marine species. *Crassostrea* and *Saccostrea* live mainly in the intertidal zone, while *Ostrea* are subtidal. The hard surfaces of oyster shells and the nooks between the shells provide places where a host of small animals can live. Hundreds of animals such as sea anemones, barnacles, and hooked mussels inhabit oyster reefs. Many of these animals are prey to larger animals, including fish such as striped bass, black drum and croakers.

An oyster reef can increase the surface area of a flat bottom 50-fold. An oyster's mature shape often depends on the type of bottom to which it is originally attached, but it always orients itself with its outer, flared shell tilted upward. One valve is cupped and the other is flat.

Oysters usually reach maturity in one year. They are protandric; during their first year they spawn as males by releasing sperm into the water. As they grow over the next two or three years and develop greater energy reserves, they spawn as females by releasing eggs. Bay oysters usually spawn by the end of June. An increase in water temperature prompts a few oysters to spawn. This triggers spawning in the rest, clouding the water with millions of eggs and sperm. A single female oyster can produce up to 100 million eggs annually. The eggs become fertilized in the water and develop into larvae, which eventually find suitable sites, such as another oyster's shell, on which to settle. Attached oyster larvae are called spat. Spat are oysters less than 25 millimetres (0.98 in) long. Many species of bivalve, oysters included, seem to be stimulated to settle near adult conspecifics.

Some tropical oysters in the family Isognomonidae grow best on mangrove roots. Low tide can expose them, making them easy to collect. In Trinidad in the West Indies, tourists are often astounded when they are told that in the Caribbean, "oysters grow on trees."

Common oyster predators include crabs, sea birds, sea stars, and humans. Some oysters contain live crabs, known as oyster crabs.

Oysters consume nitrogen-containing compounds (nitrates and ammonia), removing them from the water. Nitrogen compounds are important phytoplankton nutrients. Phytoplankton increase water turbidity. Limiting the amount of phytoplankton in the water improves water quality and other marine life by reducing competition for dissolved oxygen. Oysters feed on plankton, incidentally consuming nitrogen compounds as well. They then expel solid waste pellets which decompose into the atmosphere as nitrogen. In Maryland, the Chesapeake Bay Programme plans to use oysters to reduce the amount of nitrogen compounds entering the Chesapeake Bay by 19,000,000 pounds (8,600,000 kg) per year by 2010.

Middens testify to the prehistoric importance of oysters as food. In the United Kingdom, the town of Whitstable is noted for oyster farming from beds on the Kentish Flats that have been used since Roman times. The borough of Colchester holds an annual Oyster Feast each October, at which "Colchester Natives" (the native oyster, *Ostrea edulis*) are consumed. The United Kingdom hosts several other annual oyster festivals, for example Woburn Oyster Festival is held in September. Many breweries produce Oyster Stout, a beer intended to be drunk with oysters that sometimes includes oysters in the brewing process.

The French seaside resort of Cancale is noted for its oysters, which also date from Roman times. Sergius Orata of the Roman Republic is considered the first major merchant and cultivator of oysters. Using his considerable knowledge of hydraulics, he built a sophisticated cultivation system, including channels and locks, to control the tides. He was so famous for this that the Romans used to say he could breed oysters on the roof of his house.

The world-famous Clarenbridge and Galway Oyster Festivals take place in Galway, Ireland each September. In Ireland it is traditional to eat them live with Guinness and buttered brown soda bread.

In the early 19th century, oysters were cheap and mainly eaten by the working class. Throughout the 19th century, oyster beds in New York harbor became the largest source of oysters worldwide. On any day in the late 19th century, six million oysters could be found on barges tied up along the city's waterfront. Oysters were naturally quite popular in New York City, and helped initiate the city's restaurant trade. New York's oystermen became skilled cultivators of their beds, which provided employment for hundreds of workers and nutritious food for thousands. Eventually, rising demand exhausted many of the beds. To increase production, they introduced foreign species, which brought disease, when combined with effluent and increasing sedimentation from erosion, which destroyed most of the beds by the early 20th century. Oysters' popularity has put an ever-increasing demands on wild oyster stocks. This scarcity increased prices, converting them from their original role as working class food to their current status as an expensive delicacy.

In the United Kingdom, the native variety is still held to be the finest, requiring five years to mature and protected by an Act of Parliament during the May-August spawning season. The current market is dominated by the larger Pacific oyster and rock oyster varieties which are farmed year round.

Oysters are harvested by simply gathering them from their beds. In very shallow waters they can be gathered by hand or with small rakes. In somewhat deeper water, long-handled rakes or oyster tongs are used to reach the beds. Patent tongs can be lowered on a line to reach beds that are too deep to reach directly. In all cases the task is the same: the oysterman scrapes oysters into a pile, and then scoops them up with the rake or tongs.

In some areas a scallop dredge is used. This is a toothed bar attached to a chain bag. The dredge is towed through an oyster bed by a boat, picking up the oysters in its path. While dredges collect oysters more quickly, they heavily damage the beds, and their use is highly restricted. Until 1965 Maryland limited dredging to sailboats, and even since that date motor boats can be used only on certain days of the week. These regulations prompted the development of specialized sailboats (the bugeye and later the skipjack) for dredging.

In any case, when the oysters are collected, they are sorted to eliminate dead animals, bycatch (unwanted catch), and debris. Then they are taken to market where they are either canned or sold live.

Oysters have been cultured for well over a century. Two methods are commonly used, release and bagging. In both cases oysters are cultivated onshore to the size of spat, when they can attach themselves to a substrate. They may be allowed to mature further to form *seed oysters*. In either case they are then placed in the water to mature. The release technique involves distributing the spat throughout existing oyster beds allowing them to mature naturally to be collected like wild oysters. Bagging has the cultivator putting spat in racks or bags and keeping them above the bottom. Harvesting involves simply lifting the bags or rack to the surface and removing the mature oysters. The latter method prevents losses to some predators, but is more expensive.

The Pacific or Japanese oyster, *Crassostrea gigas* has been grown in the outflow of mariculture ponds. When fish or prawn are grown in ponds, it takes, typically 10 kilograms (22 lb) of feed to produce 1 kilogram (2.2 lb) of product (dry-

dry basis). The other 9 kilograms (20 lb) goes into the pond and after mineralization, provides food for phytoplankton, which in turn feeds the oyster.

To prevent spawning, sterile oysters are now cultured by crossbreeding tetraploid and diploid oysters. The resulting triploid oyster cannot propagate, which prevents introduced oysters from spreading into unwanted habitats.

Restoration and Recovery

In many areas non-native oysters have been introduced in attempts to prop up failing harvests of native varieties. For example, the eastern oyster was introduced to California waters in 1875, while the Pacific oyster was introduced there in 1929. Proposals for further such introductions remain controversial.

The Pacific oyster prospered in Pendrell Sound where the surface water is typically warm enough for spawning in the summer. Over the following years, spat spread out sporadically and populated adjacent areas. Eventually, possibly following adaptation to the local conditions, the Pacific oyster spread up and down the coast and now is the basis of the North American west coast oyster industry. Pendrell Sound is now a reserve that supplies spat for cultivation. Near the mouth of the Great Wicomico River in the Chesapeake Bay, five year-old artificial reefs now harbor more than 180 million native *Crassostrea virginica*. That is still a far cry from the late 1880s, when the Bay's population was in the billions, and watermen harvested about 25 million imperial bushels (910,000 m^3) annually. The 2009 harvest was less than 200,000 imperial bushels (7,300 m^3). Researchers claim that the keys to the project were:

- using waste oyster shells to elevate the reef floor 10-18 inches (0.25-0.46 m) to keep the spat free of bottom sediments.
- building larger reefs, ranging up to 20 acres (8.1 ha) in size.
- disease resistant broodstock.

Jonathan Swift is quoted as having said, "He was a bold man that first ate an oyster", but evidence of oyster consumption goes back into prehistory, evidenced by oyster middens found worldwide. Oysters were an important food source in all coastal areas where they could be found, and oyster fisheries were an important industry where they were plentiful. Overfishing and pressure from diseases and pollution have sharply reduced supplies, but they remain a popular treat celebrated in oyster festivals in many cities and towns.

There are several different types of oysters that are edible out of the over 50 different kinds that are in the oceans today.

Health Benefits of Eating Oysters

Oysters, especially 'wild', are excellent sources of several minerals, including iron, zinc and selenium, which are often low in the modern diet. They are also an excellent source of Vitamin B_{12}. Oysters are considered the healthiest when eaten raw on the half shell.

Oysters can be eaten on the half shell, raw, smoked, boiled, baked, fried, roasted, stewed, canned, pickled, steamed, broiled or used in a variety of drinks. Preparation widely varies. It can be as simple as opening the shell and eating the contents, including juice. Butter and salt are often added. In the case of oysters Rockefeller, preparation can be very elaborate. They are sometimes served on edible seaweed, such as brown algae.

Perhaps the definitive work on oysters as food is *Consider the Oyster*, by M.F.K. Fisher.

Oysters are low in food energy; one dozen raw oysters contain approximately 110 kilocalories (460 kJ), and are rich in zinc, iron, calcium, and vitamin A.

Unlike most shellfish, oysters can have a fairly long shelf-life: up to two weeks; however, their (decreasingly pleasant) taste reflects their age. Oysters should be refrigerated out of water, not frozen and in 100 per cent humidity. Oysters stored in water under refrigeration will open, consume available oxygen and die. Care should be taken when consuming oysters. Purists insist on eating them raw, with no dressing save perhaps lemon juice, vinegar (most commonly shallot vinegar), or cocktail sauce. Upscale restaurants pair raw oysters with a home-made Mignonette sauce, which consists primarily of fresh chopped shallot, mixed peppercorn, dry white wine and lemon juice or sherry vinegar. Like fine wine, raw oysters have complex flavors that vary greatly among varieties and regions: sweet, salty, earthy, or even melon. The texture is soft and fleshy, but crisp on the palate. North American varieties include: Kumamoto and Yaquina Bay from Washington State, Malpeque from Prince Edward Island, Canada, Blue Point from Long Island, New York, and Cape May oysters from New Jersey. Salinity, mineral, and nutrient variations in the water that nurtures them influence their flavor profile.

Non-local Oysters are generally expensive. In the United States, oysters are most often cooked, but there is also a high demand for raw oysters on the half-shell, or served in alcohol (*shooters*), often vodka or beer at oyster bars. Canned smoked oysters are also widely available as preserves with a long shelf life. Raw oysters are still found in many temperate areas bordering a sea or ocean. Oysters are commonly eaten raw in France in bars and as a 'bar fast food' but the home use tends to be mixed with a large usage in cooking - steamed or in paella or soups.

It was once assumed that oysters were only safe to eat in months with the letter 'r' in their English and French names. This is a myth whose basis in truth is that in the northern hemisphere oysters are much more likely to spoil in May, June, July, and August.

Oysters must be eaten alive, or cooked alive. The shells of live oysters are normally tightly closed or snap shut given a slight tap. If the shell is open, the oyster is dead, and cannot be eaten safely.

Cooking Oysters in the shell kills the oysters and causes them to open by themselves. Oysters that do not open were dead before cooking and are unsafe.

Oysters can contain harmful Bacteria. Oysters are filter feeders and will naturally concentrate anything present in the surrounding water. Oysters from the Gulf Coast of the United States, for example, contain high bacterial loads of human pathogens in the warm months, most notably *Vibrio vulnificus* and *Vibrio parahaemolyticus*. In these cases, the main danger is for immuno-compromised individuals, who are unable to fight off infection and can succumb to septicemia, leading to death. *Vibrio vulnificus* is the most deadly seafood-borne pathogen, with a higher case-to-death ratio than even *Salmonella enterica* and *Escherichia coli*.

Oysters are sometimes cited as an aphrodisiac. It is disputed whether this is true. A team of American and Italian researchers analyzed bivalves and found they were rich in rare amino acids that trigger increased levels of sex hormones. Also oysters have a high zinc content, a mineral that aids in the production of testosterone. Alternatively, the oyster's erotic reputation may only be due to its soft, moist texture and appearance.

Opening Oysters

Special knives for opening live oysters, such as this one, have short and stout blades and the best have a downward curve at the tip.

Fresh oysters must be alive just before consumption or cooking. There is only one criterion: the oyster must be capable of tightly closing its shell. Open oysters should be tapped on the shell; a live oyster will close up and is safe to eat. Oysters which are open and unresponsive are dead and must be discarded. Some dead oysters, or oyster shells which are full of sand may be closed. These make a distinctive noise when tapped, and are known as *clackers*.

Opening oysters requires skill. The preferred method is to use a special knife (called an *oyster knife*, a variant of a shucking knife), with a short and thick blade about 5 centimetres (2.0 in) long.

Insert the blade, with moderate force and vibration if necessary, at the hinge between the two valves. Then twist the blade until there is a slight pop. Then slide the blade upward to cut the adductor muscle which holds the shell closed. Inexperienced shuckers can apply too much force, which can result in injury if the blade slips. Heavy gloves are necessary: apart from the knife, the shell itself can be razor sharp. Professional shuckers require less than 3 seconds to do the deed.

If the oyster has a particularly soft shell, the knife can be inserted instead in the *sidedoor*, about halfway along one side where the oyster lips widen and there is a slight indentation.

Opening, or "shucking" oysters has become a competitive sport. Oyster shucking competitions are staged around the world. Widely acknowledged to be the premiere event, the Guinness World Oyster Opening Championship is held in September at the Galway Oyster Festival, in Galway Ireland.

Ethical Considerations

While technically an animal, the oyster is considered by some ethicists to be an appropriate food choice for vegans and vegetarians, arguing it is acceptable to eat oysters, because in the relevant *ethical* terms they are rather closer to plants than animals. Two common ethical objections to the consumption of animals is that they feel pain (and that causing pain is wrong), and that their cultivation is environmentally harmful. On both of these, oysters are significantly closer to plants than animals. Regarding pain, oysters lack a central nervous system, and do not experience pain in the same way as humans do, with them and other bivalves being closer to mobile plants than to plant perception. Regarding environmental impact, 95 per cent of oysters are sustainably farmed and harvested (other bivalves are frequently harvested by harmful dredging), feed on plankton (very low on the food chain), and in fact improve the marine environment by removing toxins. As such, oysters are listed as a "Best Choice" (highest rating) on the Seafood Watch list.

The view that oysters are acceptable to eat, even by strict ethical criteria, has notably been propounded in the seminal 1975 text *Animal Liberation,* by philosopher Peter Singer; while subsequent editions have reversed this position (advocating *against* eating oysters). Singer has stated that he has "gone back and forth on this over the years," and as of 2010 states that "unless some new evidence of a capacity for pain emerges, the doubt is so slight that there is no good reason for avoiding eating sustainably produced oysters."

Oysters are subject to various diseases which can reduce harvests and severely deplete local populations. Disease control focuses on containing infections and breeding resistant strains and is the subject of much ongoing research.

Dermo (*Perkinsus marinus*) is caused by a protozoan parasite. It is a prevalent pathogen, causes massive mortality and poses a significant economic threat to the oyster industry. The disease is not a direct threat to humans consuming infected oysters. Dermo first appeared in the Gulf of Mexico in the 1950s, and until 1978 it was believed to be caused by a fungus. While it is most serious in warmer waters, it has gradually spread up the east coast of the United States.

MSX (Multinucleated Sphere X) is caused by the protozoan *Haplosporidium nelsoni*, generally seen as a multi-nucleated plasmodium. It is infectious and causes heavy mortality in the Eastern Oyster; survivors, however, develop resistance and can help propagate resistant populations. MSX is associated with high salinity and water temperatures. MSX was first noted in Delaware Bay in 1957 and is now found all up and down the east coast of the United States. Evidence suggests that it was brought to the United States when *Crassostrea gigas*, a Japanese oyster variety, was introduced to Delaware Bay.

CHAPTER
5

Algaculture

Algaculture is a form of aquaculture involving the farming of species of algae.

The majority of algae that are intentionally cultivated fall into the category of microalgae (also referred to as phytoplankton, microphytes, or planktonic algae). Macroalgae, commonly known as seaweed, also have many commercial and industrial uses, but due to their size and the specific requirements of the environment in which they need to grow, they do not lend themselves as readily to cultivation.

Commercial and industrial algae cultivation has numerous uses, including production of food ingredients, food, fertilizer, bioplastics, dyes and colorants, chemical feedstock, pharmaceuticals, and algal fuel, and can also be used as a means of pollution control.

Most growers prefer monocultural production and go to considerable lengths to maintain the purity of their cultures. With mixed cultures, one species comes to dominate over time and if a non-dominant species is believed to have particular value, it is necessary to obtain pure cultures in order to cultivate this species. Individual species cultures are also needed for research purposes.

A common method of obtaining pure cultures is serial dilution. Cultivators dilute a wild sample or a lab sample containing the desired algae with filtered water and introduce small aliquots into a large number of small growing containers. Dilution follows a microscopic examination of the source culture that predicts that a few of the growing containers contain a single cell of the desired species. Following a suitable period on a light table, cultivators again use the microscope to identify containers to start larger cultures.

Alternatively, mixed algae cultures can work well for larval mollusks. First, the cultivator filters the sea water to remove algae which are too large for the larvae to eat. Next, the cultivator adds nutrients and possibly aerates the result. After one or two days in a greenhouse or outdoors, the resulting thin soup of mixed algae is ready for the larvae. An advantage of this method is low maintenance.

In most algal-cultivation systems, light only penetrates the top 3 to 4 inches (76-100 mm) of the water. As the algae grow and multiply, the culture becomes so dense that it blocks light from reaching deeper into the water. Direct sunlight is too strong for most algae, which need only about $^{1}/_{10}$ the amount of light they receive from direct sunlight.

To use deeper ponds, growers agitate the water, circulating the algae so that it does not remain on the surface. Paddle wheels can stir the water and compressed air coming from the bottom lifts algae from the lower regions. Agitation also helps prevent over-exposure to the sun.

Another means of supplying light is to place the light *in* the system. Glow plates made from sheets of plastic or glass and placed within the tank offer precise control over light intensity.

Odour and Oxygen

The odour associated with bogs, swamps, indeed any stagnant waters, can be due to oxygen depletion caused by the decay of deceased algal blooms. Under anoxic conditions, the bacteria inhabiting algae cultures break down the organic material and produce hydrogen sulfide and ammonia which causes the odour. This hypoxia often results in the death of aquatic animals. In a system where algae is intentionally cultivated, maintained, and harvested, neither eutrophication nor hypoxia are likely to occur.

Some living algae also produce odourous chemicals, particularly certain blue-green algae (cyanobacteria) such as *Anabaena*. The most well-known of these odour-causing chemicals are MIB (2-methylisoborneol) and geosmin. They give a musty or earthy odour that can be quite strong. Eventual death of the cyanobacteria releases additional gas that is trapped in the cells. These chemicals are detectable at very low levels, in the parts per billion range, and are responsible for many "taste and odour" issues in drinking water treatment and distribution. Cyanobacteria can also produce chemical toxins that have been a problem in drinking water.

Open-ponds

Raceway-type ponds and lakes are open to the elements. Open ponds are highly vulnerable to contamination by other microorganisms, such as other algal species or bacteria. Thus cultivators usually choose closed systems for monocultures. Open systems also do not offer control over temperature and lighting. The growing season is largely dependent on location and, aside from tropical areas, is limited to the warmer months.

Open pond systems are cheaper to construct, at the minimum requiring only a trench or pond. Large ponds have the largest production capacities relative to other systems of comparable cost. Also, open pond cultivation can exploit unusual conditions that suit only specific algae. For instance,

Spirulina sp. thrives in water with a high concentration of sodium bicarbonate and *Dunaliella salina* grow in extremely salty water. Open culture can also work if there is a system of culling the desired algae and inoculating new ponds with a high starting concentration of the desired algae.

Some chain diatoms fall into this category since they can be filtered from a stream of water flowing through an outflow pipe. A "pillow case" of a fine mesh cloth is tied over the outflow pipe allowing other algae to escape. The chain diatoms are held in the bag and feed shrimp larvae (in Eastern hatcheries) and inoculate new tanks or ponds.

Enclosing a pond with a transparent or translucent barrier effectively turns it into a greenhouse. This solves many of the problems associated with an open system. It allows more species to be grown; it allows the species that are being grown to stay dominant; and it extends the growing season – and if heated the pond can produce year round.

Photobioreactors

Algae can also be grown in a photobioreactor (PBR). A PBR is a bioreactor which incorporates a light source. Virtually any translucent container could be called a PBR, however the term is more commonly used to define a closed system, as opposed to an open tank or pond.

Because PBR systems are closed, the cultivator must provide all nutrients, including CO_2.

A PBR can operate in "batch mode", which involves restocking the reactor after each harvest, but it is also possible to grow and harvest continuously. Continuous operation requires precise control of all elements to prevent immediate collapse. The grower provides sterilized water, nutrients, air, and carbon dioxide at the correct rates. This allows the reactor to operate for long periods. An advantage is that algae that grows in the "log phase" is generally of higher nutrient content than old "senescent" algae. Maximum productivity occurs when the "exchange rate" (time to exchange one volume of liquid) is equal to the "doubling time" (in mass or volume) of the algae.

Different types of PBRs include:

- tanks
- Polyethylene sleeves or bags
- Glass or plastic tubes.

Harvesting

Algae can be harvested using microscreens, by centrifugation, by flocculation. and by froth flotation.

Interrupting the carbon dioxide supply can cause algae to flocculate on its own, which is called "autoflocculation".

"Chitosan", a commercial flocculant, more commonly used for water purification, is far more expensive. The powdered shells of crustaceans are processed to acquire chitin, a polysaccharide found in the shells, from which chitosan is derived via de-acetylation. Water that is more brackish, or saline requires larger amounts of flocculant. Flocculation is often too expensive for large operations.

Alum and ferric chloride are other chemical flocculants.

In froth flotation, the cultivator aerates the water into a froth, and then skims the algae from the top.

Ultrasound and other harvesting methods are currently under development.

Oil Extraction

Algae oils have a variety of commercial and industrial uses, and are extracted through a wide variety of methods. Estimates of the cost to extract oil from microalgae vary, but are likely to be around $1.80 (US$)/kg (compared to $0.50 (US$)/kg for palm oil).

Physical Extraction

In the first step of extraction, the oil must be separated from the rest of the algae. The simplest method is mechanical crushing. When algae is dried it retains its oil content, which then can be "pressed" out with an oil press. Many commercial manufacturers of vegetable oil use a combination of mechanical pressing and chemical solvents in extracting oil. Since different strains of algae vary widely in their physical attributes, various press configurations (screw, expeller, piston, etc.) work better for specific algae types.

Osmotic shock is a sudden reduction in osmotic pressure, this can cause cells in a solution to rupture. Osmotic shock is sometimes used to release cellular components, such as oil.

Ultrasonic extraction, a branch of sonochemistry, can greatly accelerate extraction processes. Using an ultrasonic reactor, ultrasonic waves are used to create cavitation bubbles in a solvent material. When these bubbles collapse near the cell walls, the resulting shock waves and liquid jets cause those cells walls to break and release their contents into a solvent. Ultrasonication can enhance basic enzymatic extraction. The combination "sonoenzymatic treatment" accelerates extraction and increases yields.

Chemical Extraction

Chemical solvents are often used in the extraction of the oils. The downside to using solvents for oil extraction are the dangers involved in working with the chemicals. Care must be taken to avoid exposure to vapors and skin contact, either of which can cause serious health damage. Chemical solvents also present an explosion hazard.

A common choice of chemical solvent is hexane, which is widely used in the food industry and is relatively inexpensive. Benzene and ether can also separate oil. Benzene is classified as a carcinogen.

Another method of chemical solvent extraction is Soxhlet extraction. In this method, oils from the algae are extracted through repeated washing, or percolation, with an organic solvent such as hexane or petroleum ether, under reflux in a special glassware. The value of this technique is that the solvent is reused for each cycle.

Enzymatic extraction uses enzymes to degrade the cell walls with water acting as the solvent. This makes fractionation of the oil much easier. The costs of this extraction process are estimated to be much greater than hexane extraction. The enzymatic extraction can be supported by ultrasonication. The combination "sonoenzymatic treatment" causes faster extraction and higher oil yields.

Supercritical CO_2 can also be used as a solvent. In this method, CO_2 is liquefied under pressure and heated to the point that it becomes supercritical (having properties of both a liquid and a gas), allowing it to act as a solvent.

Other methods are still being developed, including ones to extract specific types of oils, such as those with a high production of long-chain highly unsaturated fatty acids.

Purple laver (*Porphyra*) is perhaps the most widely domesticated marine algea. In Asia it is used in nori (Japan) and gim (Korea). In Wales, it is used in laverbread, a traditional food, and in Ireland it is collected and made into a jelly by stewing or boiling. Preparation also can involve frying or heating the fronds with a little water and beating with a fork to produce a pinkish jelly. Harvesting also occurs along the west coast of North America, and in Hawaii and New Zealand.

Dulse (*Palmaria palmata*) is a red species sold in Ireland and Atlantic Canada. It is eaten raw, fresh, dried, or cooked like spinach.

Spirulina (*Arthrospira platensis*) is a blue-green microalgae with a long history as a food source in East Africa and pre-colonial Mexico. Spirulina is high in protein and other nutrients, finding use as a food supplement and for malnutrition. Spirulina thrives in open systems and commercial growers have found it well-suited to cultivation. One of the largest production sites is Lake Texcoco in central Mexico. The plants produce a variety of nutrients and high amounts of protein. Spirulina is often used commercially as a nutritional supplement.

Chlorella, another popular microalgae, has similar nutrition to spirulina. Chlorella is very popular in Japan. It is also used as a nutritional supplement with possible effects on metabolic rate. Some allege that Chlorella can reduce mercury levels in humans (supposedly by chelation of the mercury to the cell wall of the organism).

Irish moss (*Chondrus crispus*), often confused with *Mastocarpus stellatus*, is the source of carrageenan, which is used as a stiffening agent in instant puddings, sauces, and dairy products such as ice cream. Irish moss is also used by beer brewers as a fining agent.

Sea lettuce (*Ulva lactuca*), is used in Scotland where it is added to soups and salads. Dabberlocks or badderlocks (*Alaria esculenta*) is eaten either fresh or cooked in Greenland, Iceland, Scotland and Ireland.

Aphanizomenon flos-aquae is a cyanobacteria similar to spirulina, which is used as a nutitional supplement.

Extracts and oils from algae are also used as additives in various food products. The plants also produce Omega-3 and Omega-6 fatty acids, which are commonly found in fish oils, and which have been shown to have positive health benefits.

Sargassum species are an important group of seaweeds. These algae have many phlorotannins.

Fertilizer and Agar

For centuries seaweed has been used as fertilizer. It is also an excellent source of potassium for manufacture of potash and potassium nitrate.

Both microalgae and macroalgae are used to make agar.

Pollution Control

With concern over global warming, new methods for the thorough and efficient capture of CO_2 are being sought out. The carbon dioxide that a carbon-fuel burning plant produces can feed into open or closed algae systems, fixing the CO_2 and accelerating algae growth. Untreated sewage can supply additional nutrients, thus turning two pollutants into valuable commodities.

Algae cultivation is under study for uranium/plutonium sequestration and purifying fertilizer runoff.

Energy Production

Business, academia and governments are exploring the possibility of using algae to make gasoline, diesel and other fuels.

Other Uses

Chlorella, particularly a transgenic strain which carries an extra mercury reductase gene, has been studied as an agent for environmental remediation due to its ability to reduce Hg^{2+} to the less toxic elemental mercury.

Cultivated algae serve many other purposes, including bioplastic production, dyes and colorant production, chemical feedstock production, and pharmaceutical ingredients. AF^-.

Algae (pronounced singular *alga* Latin for "seaweed") are a large and diverse group of simple, typically autotrophic organisms, ranging from unicellular to multicellular forms, such as the giant kelps that grow to 65 meters in length. The U.S. Algal Collection is represented by almost 300,000 accessioned and inventoried herbarium specimens. The largest and most complex marine forms are called seaweeds. They are photosynthetic like plants, and "simple" because their tissues are not organized into the many distinct organs found in land plants.

Though the prokaryotic cyanobacteria (commonly referred to as blue-green algae) were traditionally included as "algae" in older textbooks, many modern sources regard this as outdated as they are now considered to be bacteria. The term *algae* is now restricted to eukaryotic organisms. All true algae therefore have a nucleus enclosed within a membrane and plastids bound in one or more membranes. Algae constitute a paraphyletic and polyphyletic group, as they do not include all the descendants of the last universal ancestor nor do they all descend from a common algal ancestor, although their plastids seem to have a single origin. Diatoms are also examples of algae.

Algae are found in the fossil record dating back to approximately 3 billion years in the Precambrian. They exhibit a wide range of reproductive strategies, from simple, asexual cell division to complex forms of sexual reproduction.

Algae lack the various structures that characterize land plants, such as phyllids (leaves) and rhizoids in nonvascular plants, or leaves, roots, and other organs that are found in tracheophytes (vascular plants). Many are photoautotrophic, although some groups contain members that are mixotrophic, deriving energy both from photosynthesis and uptake of organic carbon either by osmotrophy, myzotrophy, or phagotrophy. Some unicellular species rely entirely on external energy sources and have limited or no photosynthetic apparatus.

Nearly all algae have photosynthetic machinery ultimately derived from the Cyanobacteria, and so produce oxygen as a by-product of photosynthesis, unlike other photosynthetic bacteria such as purple and green sulfur bacteria. Fossilized filamentous algae from the Vindhya basin have been dated back to 1.6 to 1.7 billion years ago.

The singular *alga* is the Latin word for a particular seaweed and retains that meaning in English. The etymology is obscure. Although some speculate that it is related to Latin *algere,* "be cold", there is no known reason to associate seaweed with temperature. A more likely source is *alliga,* "binding, entwining." Since Algae has become a biological classification, alga can also mean one classification under Algae, parallel to a fungus being a species of fungi, a plant being a species of plant, and so on.

The ancient Greek word for seaweed was *fukos* or *phykos,* which could mean either the seaweed, probably Red Algae, or a red dye derived from it. The Latinization, *fucus,* meant primarily the cosmetic rouge. The etymology is uncertain, but a strong candidate has long been some word related to the Biblical *puk,* "paint" (if not that word itself), a cosmetic eye-shadow used by the ancient Egyptians and other inhabitants of the eastern Mediterranean. It could be any colour: black, red, green, blue.

Accordingly the modern study of marine and freshwater algae is called either phycology or algology. The name Fucus appears in a number of taxa. The singular form is alga.

While *Cyanobacteria* have been traditionally included among the Algae, recent works usually exclude them due to large differences such as the lack of membrane-bound organelles, the presence of a single circular chromosome, the presence of peptidoglycan in the cell walls, and ribosomes different in size and content from those of the Eukaryotes. Rather than in chloroplasts, they conduct photosynthesis on specialized infolded cytoplasmic membranes called thylakoid membranes. Therefore, they differ significantly from the Algae despite occupying similar ecological niches.

By modern definitions: Algae are Eukaryotes and conduct photosynthesis within membrane-bound organelles called chloroplasts. Chloroplasts contain circular DNA and are similar in structure to Cyanobacteria, presumably representing reduced cyanobacterial endosymbionts. The exact nature of the chloroplasts is different among the different lines of Algae, reflecting different endosymbiotic events. The table below describes the composition of the three major groups of Algae. Their lineage relationships are shown in the figure in the upper right. Many of these groups contain some members that are no longer photosynthetic. Some retain plastids, but not chloroplasts, while others have lost plastids entirely. The singular form is alga.

The first plants on earth evolved from shallow freshwater algae much like *Chara* some 400 million years ago. These probably had an isomorphic alternation of generations and were probably filamentous. Fossils of isolated land plant spores suggest land plants may have been around as long as 475 million years ago.

Morphology

A range of algal morphologies are exhibited, and convergence of features in unrelated groups is common. The only groups to exhibit three dimensional multicellular thalli are the reds and browns, and some chlorophytes. Apical growth is constrained to subsets of these groups: the florideophyte reds, various browns, and the charophytes. The form of charophytes is quite different to those of reds and browns, because have distinct nodes, separated by internode 'stems'; whorls of branches reminiscent of the horsetails occur at the nodes. Conceptacles are another polyphyletic trait; they appear in the coralline algae and the Hildenbrandiales, as well as the browns.

Most of the simpler algae are unicellular flagellates or amoeboids, but colonial and non-motile forms have developed independently among several of the groups. Some of the more common organizational levels, more than one of which may occur in the life cycle of a species, are:

- *Colonial*: small, regular groups of motile cells
- *Capsoid*: individual non-motile cells embedded in mucilage
- *Coccoid*: individual non-motile cells with cell walls
- *Palmelloid*: non-motile cells embedded in mucilage
- *Filamentous*: a string of non-motile cells connected together, sometimes branching
- *Parenchymatous*: cells forming a hallus with partial differentiation of tissues

In three lines even higher levels of organization have been reached, with full tissue differentiation. These are the brown algae,—some of which may reach 50 m in length (kelps)—the red algae, and the green algae. The most complex forms are found among the green algae (see Charales and Charophyta), in a lineage that eventually led to the higher land plants. The point where these non-algal plants begin and algae stop is usually taken to be the presence of reproductive organs with protective cell layers, a characteristic not found in the other alga groups.

Symbiotic Algae

Some species of algae form symbiotic relationships with other organisms. In these symbioses, the algae supply photosynthates (organic substances) to the host organism providing protection to the algal cells. The host organism derives some or all of its energy requirements from the algae. Examples are as follows:

Lichens are defined by the International Association for Lichenology to be "an association of a fungus and a photosynthetic symbiont resulting in a stable vegetative body having a specific structure." The fungi, or mycobionts, are from the Ascomycota with a few from the Basidiomycota. They are not found alone in nature but when they began to associate is not known. One mycobiont associates with the same phycobiont species, rarely two, from the Green Algae, except that alternatively the mycobiont may associate with the same species of Cyanobacteria (hence "photobiont" is the more accurate term). A photobiont may be associated with many specific mycobionts or live independently; accordingly, lichens are named and classified as fungal species. The association is termed a morphogenesis because the lichen has a form and capabilities not possessed by the symbiont species alone (they can be experimentally isolated). It is possible that the photobiont triggers otherwise latent genes in the mycobiont.

Coral Reefs

Coral reefs are accumulated from the calcareous exoskeletons of marine invertebrates of the Scleractinia order; i.e., the Stony Corals. As animals they metabolize sugar and oxygen to obtain energy for their cell-building processes, including secretion of the exoskeleton, with water and carbon dioxide as byproducts. As the reef is the result of a favorable equilibrium between construction by the corals and destruction by marine erosion, the rate at which metabolism can proceed determines the growth or deterioration of the reef.

Algae of the *Dinoflagellate phylum* are often endosymbionts in the cells of marine invertebrates, where they accelerate host-cell metabolism by generating immediately available sugar and oxygen through photosynthesis using incident light and the carbon dioxide produced in the host. Endosymbiont algae in the Stony Corals are described by the term zooxanthellae, with the host Stony Corals called on that account hermatypic corals, which although not a taxon are not in healthy condition without their endosymbionts. Zooxanthellae belong almost entirely to the genus *Symbiodinium*. The loss of *Symbiodinium* from the host is known as coral bleaching, a condition which unless corrected leads to the deterioration and loss of the reef.

Sea Sponges

Green Algae live close to the surface of some sponges, for example, breadcrumb sponge (*Halichondria panicea*). The alga is thus protected from predators; the sponge is provided with oxygen and sugars which can account for 50 to 80 per cent of sponge growth in some species.

Life-cycle

Rhodophyta, Chlorophyta and Heterokontophyta, the three main algal Phyla, have life-cycles which show tremendous variation with considerable complexity. In general there is an asexual phase where the seaweed's cells are diploid, a sexual phase where the cells are haploid followed by fusion of the male and female gametes. Asexual reproduction is advantageous in that it permits efficient population increases, but less variation is possible. Sexual reproduction allows more variation, but is more costly. Often there is no strict alternation between the sporophyte and also because there is often an asexual phase, which could include the fragmentation of the thallus.

The *Algal Collection of the U.S. National Herbarium* (located in the National Museum of Natural History) consists of approximately 320500 dried specimens, which, although not exhaustive (no exhaustive collection exists), gives an idea of the order of magnitude of the number of algal species (that number remains unknown). Estimates vary widely. For example, according to one standard textbook, in the British Isles the *U.K. Biodiversity Steering Group Report* estimated there to be 20000 algal species in the U.K. Another checklist reports only about 5000 species. Regarding the difference of about 15000 species, the text concludes: "It will require many detailed field surveys before it is possible to provide a reliable estimate of the total number of species ...."

Regional and group estimates have been made as well: 5000-5500 species of Red Algae worldwide, "some 1300 in Australian Seas," 400 seaweed species for the western coastline of South Africa, 669 marine species from California (U.S.A.), 642 in the check-list of Britain and Ireland, and so on, but lacking any scientific basis or reliable sources, these numbers have no more credibility than the British ones mentioned above. Most estimates also omit the microscopic Algae, such as the phytoplankta, entirely.

Distribution

The topic of distribution of algal species has been fairly well studied since the founding of phytogeography in the mid-19th century AD. Algae spread mainly by the dispersal of spores analogously to the dispersal of Plantae by seeds and spores. Spores are everywhere in all parts of the Earth: the waters fresh and marine, the atmosphere, free-floating and in precipitation or mixed with dust, the humus and in other organisms, such as humans. Whether a spore is to grow into an organism depends on the combination of the species and the environmental conditions of where the spore lands.

The spores of fresh-water Algae are dispersed mainly by running water and wind, as well as by living carriers. The bodies of water into which they are transported are chemically selective. Marine spores are spread by currents. Ocean water is temperature selective, resulting in phytogeographic zones, regions and provinces.

To some degree the distribution of Algae is subject to floristic discontinuities caused by geographical features, such as Antarctica, long distances of ocean or general land masses.

It is therefore possible to identify species occurring by locality, such as "Pacific Algae" or "North Sea Algae". When they occur out of their localities, it is usually possible to hypothesize a transport mechanism, such as the hulls of ships. For example, *Ulva reticulata* and *Ulva fasciata* travelled from the mainland to Hawaii in this manner.

Mapping is possible for select species only: "there are many valid examples of confined distribution patterns." For example, *Clathromorphum* is an arctic genus and is not mapped far south of there. On the other hand, scientists regard the overall data as insufficient due to the "difficulties of undertaking such studies".

For centuries seaweed has been used as a fertilizer; George Owen of Henllys writing in the 16th century referring to drift weed in South Wales:

This kind of ore they often gather and lay on great heapes, where it heteth and rotteth, and will have a strong and loathsome smell; when being so rotten they cast on the land, as they do their muck, and thereof springeth good corn, especially barley ... After spring-tydes or great rigs of the sea, they fetch it in sacks on horse backes, and carie the same three, four, or five miles, and cast it on the lande, which doth very much better the ground for corn and grass.

Today Algae are used by humans in many ways; for example, as fertilizers, soil conditioners and livestock feed. Aquatic and microscopic species are cultured in clear tanks or ponds and are either harvested or used to treat effluents pumped through the ponds. Algaculture on a large scale is an important type of aquaculture in some places. Maerl is commonly used as a soil conditioner.

Algae are prominent in bodies of water, common in terrestrial environments and are found in unusual environments, such as on snow and on ice. Seaweeds grow mostly in shallow marine waters, under 100 metres (330 ft); however some have been recorded to a depth of 360 metres (1,180 ft).

The various sorts of algae play significant roles in aquatic ecology. Microscopic forms that live suspended in the water column (phytoplankton) provide the food base for most marine food chains. In very high densities (algal blooms) these algae may discolor the water and outcompete, poison, or asphyxiate other life forms.

Algae are variously sensitive to different factors, which has made them useful as biological indicators in the Ballantine Scale and its modification.

Naturally growing seaweeds are an important source of food, especially in Asia. They provide many vitamins including: A, B_1, B_2, B_6, niacin and C, and are rich in iodine, potassium, iron, magnesium and calcium. In addition commercially cultivated microalgae, including both Algae and Cyanobacteria, are marketed as nutritional supplements, such as Spirulina, Chlorella and the Vitamin-C supplement, Dunaliella, high in beta-carotene.

Algae are national foods of many nations: China consumes more than 70 species, including *fat choy*, a cyanobacterium considered a vegetable; Japan, over 20 species; Ireland, dulse; Chile, cochayuyo. Laver is used to make "laver bread" in Wales where it is known as *bara lawr*; in Korea, gim; in Japan, nori and aonori. It is also used along the west coast of North America from California to British Columbia, in Hawaii and by the Maori of New Zealand. Sea lettuce and badderlocks are a salad ingredient in Scotland, Ireland, Greenland and Iceland.

The oils from some Algae have high levels of unsaturated fatty acids. For example, *Parietochloris incisa* is very high in arachidonic acid, where it reaches up to 47 per cent of the triglyceride pool. Some varieties of Algae favored by vegetarianism and veganism contain the long-chain, essential omega-3 fatty acids, Docosahexaenoic acid (DHA) and Eicosapentaenoic acid (EPA), in addition to vitamin B_{12}. The vitamin B_{12} in algae is not biologically active. Fish oil contains the omega-3 fatty acids, but the original source is algae (microalgae in particular), which are eaten by marine life such as copepods and are passed up the food chain. Algae has emerged in recent years as a popular source of omega-3 fatty acids for vegetarians who cannot get long-chain EPA and DHA from other vegetarian sources such as flaxseed oil, which only contains the short-chain Alpha-Linolenic acid.

Sewage can be treated with algae, reducing the need for greater amounts of toxic chemicals than are already used.

Algae can be used to capture fertilizers in runoff from farms. When subsequently harvested, the enriched algae itself can be used as fertilizer.

Agricultural Research Service scientists found that 60-90 per cent of nitrogen runoff and 70-100 per cent of phosphorus runoff can be captured from manure effluents using an algal turf scrubber (ATS). Scientists developed the ATS, which are shallow, 100-foot raceways of nylon netting where algae colonies can form, and studied its efficacy for three years. They found that algae can readily be used to reduce the nutrient runoff from agricultural fields and increase the quality of water flowing into rivers, streams, and oceans. The enriched algae itself also can be used as a fertilizer. Researchers collected and dried the nutrient-rich algae from the ATS and studied its potential as an organic fertilizer. They found that cucumber and corn seedlings grew just as well using ATS organic fertilizer as they did with commercial fertilizers.

CHAPTER 6

Fishkeeping

Fishkeeping is a popular hobby concerned with keeping fish in a home aquarium or garden pond. There is also a fishkeeping industry, as a branch of agriculture.

Fishkeepers are often known as "aquarists", since many of them are not solely interested in keeping fish. The hobby can be broadly divided into three specific disciplines according to the type of water the fish tolerate: freshwater, brackish, and marine (also called saltwater) fishkeeping.

Freshwater

Freshwater fishkeeping is by far the most popular branch of the hobby, with even small pet stores often selling a variety of freshwater fish, such as goldfish, guppies, and angelfish. While most freshwater aquaria are community tanks containing a variety of compatible species, single-species breeding aquaria are also popular. Livebearing fish such as mollies and guppies are among those most easily raised in captivity, but aquarists also regularly breed many types of cichlid, catfish, characin, and killifish.

Many fishkeepers create freshwater aquascapes where the focus is on aquatic plants as well as fish. These aquaria include "Dutch Aquaria", named for European aquarists who designed them. In recent years, one of the most active advocates of the heavily planted aquarium is the Japanese aquarist Takashi Amano.

Garden ponds are in some ways similar to freshwater aquaria, but are usually much larger and exposed to ambient weather. In the tropics, tropical fish can be kept in garden ponds, but in the temperate zone species such as goldfish, koi, and orfe work better.

Saltwater

Marine aquaria are generally more difficult to maintain and the livestock is significantly more expensive. As a result this branch tends to attract more experienced fishkeepers. Marine aquaria can be exceedingly beautiful, due to the attractive colors and shapes of the corals and the coral reef fishthey host. Temperate zone marine fish are not as commonly kept in home aquaria, primarily because they do not thrive at room temperature. Coldwater aquaria must provide cooler temperature via a cool room (such as an unheated basement) or a refrigeration device known as a 'chiller'.

Marine aquarists often attempt to recreate a coral reef in their aquaria using large quantities of living rock, porous calcareous rocks encrusted with coralline algae, sponges, worms, and other small marine organisms. Larger corals as well as shrimps, crabs, echinoderms, and mollusks are added later on, once the aquarium has matured, as well as a variety of small fish. Such aquaria are sometimes called reef tanks.

Brackish Water

Brackish water aquaria combine elements of the other types, with salinity that must stay between that of freshwater and seawater. Brackish water fish come from habitats with varying salinity, such as mangroves and estuaries, and do not thrive if kept permanently in freshwater. Although brackish water aquaria are not necessarily familiar to inexperienced aquarists, many species prefer brackish water, including some mollies, many gobies, some pufferfish, monos, scats, and virtually all the freshwater soles.

Fish have been raised as food in pools and ponds for thousands of years. Brightly colored or tame specimens of fish in these pools have sometimes been valued as pets rather than food. Many other cultures kept fish for both functional and decorative purposes.

Ancient Sumerians kept wild-caught fish in ponds, before preparing them for meals. Depictions of the sacred fish of Oxyrhynchus kept in captivity in rectangular temple pools have been found in ancient Egyptian art.

Similarly, Asia has experienced a long history of stocking rice paddies with freshwater fish suitable for eating, including various types of catfish and cyprinid. Selective breeding of carp into today's popular and completely domesticated koi and goldfish began over 2,000 years ago in Japan and China, respectively. The Chinese brought goldfish indoors during the Song Dynasty to enjoy them in large ceramic vessels.

In Medieval Europe, carp pools were a standard feature of estates and monasteries, providing an alternative to meat on feast days when meat could not be eaten for religious reasons.

Marine fish have been similarly valued for centuries. Wealthy Romans kept lampreys and other fish in salt water pools. Tertullian reports that Asinius Celer paid 8000 sesterces for a particularly fine mullet. Cicero reports that the advocate Quintus Hortensius wept when a favored specimen died. Rather cynically, he referred to these ancient fishkeepers as the Piscinarii, the "fish-pond owners" or "fish breeders", for example when saying that *...the rich (I mean your friends the fish-breeders) did not disguise their jealousy of me.*

Ideal aquarium ecology reproduces the balance found in nature in the closed system of an aquarium. In practice it is virtually impossible to maintain a perfect balance. As an example, a balanced predator-prey relationship is nearly impossible to maintain in even the largest aquaria. Typically, an aquarium keeper must actively maintain balance in the small ecosystems that aquaria provide.

Balance is facilitated by larger volumes of water which dilute the effects of a systemic shock. For example, the death of the only fish in a 10 litres (2.2 imp gal; 2.6 US gal) tank causes dramatic changes in the system, while the death of that same fish in a 400 litres (88 imp gal; 110 US gal) tank that holds many fish creates only a minor imbalance. For this reason, hobbyists often favor larger tanks when possible, as they require less intensive attention.

A variety of nutrient cycles are important in the aquarium. Dissolved oxygen enters at the surface water-air interface or through the actions of an air pump. Carbon dioxide escapes into the air. The phosphate cycle is an important, although often overlooked, nutrient cycle. Sulfur, iron, and micronutrients enter the system as food and exit as waste. Appropriate handling of the nitrogen cycle, along with a balanced food supply and consideration of biological loading, is usually enough to keep these nutrient cycles in adequate equilibrium.

Water Conditions

The solute content of water is perhaps the most important aspect of water conditions, as total dissolved solids and other constituents can dramatically impact basic water chemistry, and therefore how organisms interact with their environment. Salt content, or salinity, is the most basic classification of water conditions. An aquarium may have freshwater (salinity below 0.5 PPT), simulating a lake or river environment; brackish water (a salt level of 0.5 to 30 PPT), simulating environments lying between fresh and salt, such as estuaries; and salt water or seawater (a salt level of 30 to 40 PPT), simulating an ocean or sea environment. Even higher salt concentrations are maintained in specialized tanks for raising brine organisms.

Several other water characteristics result from dissolved materials in the water, and are important to the proper simulation of natural environments. Saltwater is typically alkaline, while the pH of fresh water varies. "Hardness" measures overall dissolved mineral content; hard or soft water may be preferred. Hard water is usually alkaline, while soft water is usually neutral to acidic. Dissolved organic content and dissolved gases content are also important factors.

Home aquarists typically use modified tap water supplied through their local water supply network. Because of the chlorine used to disinfect drinking water supplies for human consumption, tap water cannot be immediately used. In the past, it was possible to "condition" the water by simply letting the water stand for a day or two, which allows the chlorine to dissipate. However, chloramine became popular in water treatment because it stays longer in the water. Additives are available to remove chlorine or chloramine and suffice to make the water ready. Brackish or saltwater aquaria require the addition of a mixture of salts and other minerals.

More sophisticated aquarists may modify the water's alkalinity, hardness, or dissolved content of organics and gases. This can be accomplished by additives such as sodium bicarbonate to raise pH. Some aquarists filter or purify their water using one of two processes: deionization or reverse osmosis. In contrast, public aquaria with large water needs often locate themselves near a natural water source (such as a river, lake, or ocean) in order to have easy access to water that requires only minimal treatment.

Water temperature forms the basis of one of the two most basic aquarium classifications: tropical vs. cold water. Most fish and plant species tolerate only a limited range of water temperatures: Tropical or warm water aquaria maintain an average temperature of about 25°C (77°F) are much more common, and tropical fish are among the most popular aquarium denizens. Cold water aquaria maintain temperatures below the room temperature. More importantly than the range is temperature consistency; most organisms are not accustomed to sudden changes in temperatures, which can cause shock and lead to disease. Water temperature can be regulated with a combined thermometer and heating or cooling unit.

Water movement can also be important in accurately simulating a natural ecosystem. Fish may prefer anything from still water up to swift, simulated currents. Water movement can be controlled through the use of aeration from air pumps, powerheads, and careful design of water flow (such as location of filtration system points of inflow and outflow).

Nitrogen Cycle

Fish are animals and generate waste as they metabolize food, which aquarists must manage. Fish, invertebrates, fungi, and some bacteria excrete nitrogen in the form of ammonia (which converts to ammonium in acidic water) and must then pass through the nitrogen cycle. Ammonia is also produced through the decomposition of plant and animal matter, including fecal matter and other detritus. Nitrogen waste products become toxic to fish and other aquarium inhabitants above a certain concentration.

The Process

A well-balanced tank contains organisms that metabolize the waste products of other inhabitants. Nitrogen waste is metabolized in aquaria by a type of bacteria known as nitrifiers (genus *Nitrosomonas*). Nitrifying bacteria metabolize ammonia into nitrite. Nitrite is also highly toxic to fish in high concentrations. Another type of bacteria, genus *Nitrospira,* on–converts nitrite into less–toxic nitrate. (*Nitrobacter* bacteria were previously believed to fill this role, and appear in "jump start" kits. While biologically they could theoretically fill the same niche as Nitrospira, it has recently been found that *Nitrobacter* are not present in detectable levels in established aquaria, while *Nitrospira* are plentiful.) This process is known in the aquarium hobby as the nitrogen cycle.

Aquatic plants also metabolize ammonia and nitrate, using it to build biomass. However, this is only temporary, as the plants release nitrogen back into the water when older leaves die off and decompose.

Maintaining the Nitrogen Cycle

Although called the nitrogen "cycle" by hobbyists, in aquaria the cycle is not complete: nitrogen must be added (usually indirectly through food) and nitrates must be removed at the end. Nitrogen bound up in plant matter is removed when the plant grows too large.

Hobbyist aquaria typically do not have the requisite bacteria needed to detoxify nitrogen waste. This problem is most often addressed through filtration. Activated carbon filters absorb nitrogen compounds and other toxins from the water.

Biological filters provide a medium specially designed for colonization by the desired nitrifying bacteria. Activated carbon and other substances, such as ammonia absorbing resins, stop working when their pores fill, so these components have to be replaced with fresh stocks periodically.

New aquaria often have problems associated with the nitrogen cycle due to insufficient beneficial bacteria, which is known as "New Tank Syndrome". Therefore, new tanks have to mature before stocking them with fish. There are three basic approaches to this: the *fishless cycle*, the *silent cycle*, and *slow growth*.

Tanks undergoing a "fishless cycle" have no fish. Instead, the keeper adds ammonia to feed the bacteria. During this process, ammonia, nitrite, and nitrate levels measure progress.

The "silent cycle" involves adding fast-growing plants and relying on them to consume the nitrogen, filling in for the bacteria work until their number increases. Anecdotal reports indicate that such plants can consume nitrogenous waste so efficiently that the ammonia and nitrite spikes that occur in more traditional cycling methods are greatly reduced or indetectable.

"Slow growth" entails slowly increasing the fish population over 6 to 8 weeks, giving bacteria time to grow and reach a balance with the increasing waste production.

The largest bacterial populations inhabit the filter; efficient filtration is vital. Sometimes, simply cleaning the filter is enough to seriously disturb the aquarium's balance. Best practice is to flush mechanical filters using compatible water to dislodge organic materials, while preserving bacteria populations. Another safe practice involves cleaning only one half of the filter media every time the filter or filters are serviced to allow the remaining bacteria to repopulate the cleaned half.

Tank Capacity

Biological loading is a measure of the burden placed on the aquarium ecosystem by its living inhabitants. Higher biological loading represents a more complicated ecology, which makes equilibrium easier to perturb. The surface area of water exposed to air limits dissolved oxygen.The population of nitrifying bacteria is limited by the available physical space.

Tank Size

Fish capacity is a function of aquarium size. Limiting factors include the availability of oxygen in the water and the rate at which the filter can process waste. Aquarists apply rules of thumb estimating appropriate population size; the examples below are for small freshwater fish. Larger freshwater fish and most marine fishes need much more generous allowances. Some aquarists claim that increasing water depth beyond some relatively shallow minimum does not affect capacity.

- 1.5 of water for each centimetre of fish length (1 gallon per inch).
- 30 square centimetres of surface area per centimetre of fish length (12 square inches per inch).

Experienced aquarists warn against mechanically applying these rules because they do not consider other important issues such as growth rate, activity level, social behaviour, and so on. Once the tank nears capacity, best practice is to add the remaining fish over a period of time while monitoring water quality.

The capacity can be improved by surface movement and water circulation such as through aeration, which not only improves oxygen exchange, but also the decomposition of waste materials.

Other Factors

Other variables affect tank capacity. Smaller fish consume more oxygen per unit of body weight than larger fish. Labyrinth fish can breathe atmospheric oxygen and need less surface area (however, some are territorial, and do not tolerate crowding). Barbs require more surface area than tetras of comparable size. The presence of waste materials presents itself as a variable as well. Decomposition consumes oxygen, reducing the amount available for fish. Oxygen dissolves less readily in warmer water, while warmer water temperature increase fish activity levels, which in turn consume more oxygen.

Fishkeeping Industry

Worldwide, the fishkeeping hobby is a multi-billion dollar industry. The United States is the largest market, followed by Europe and Japan. In 1993 the United States Census Bureau found that 10.6 per cent of U.S. households owned ornamental freshwater or saltwater fish, with an average of 8.8 fish per household. In 1993, the retail value of the fish hobby in the United States was US$910 million. In 2002, census data indicated that aquarium products and fished accounted for USD684 million dolllars.

From 1989 to 1992, almost 79 per cent of all U.S. ornamental fish imports came from Southeast Asia and Japan. Singapore, Thailand, the Philippines, Hong Kong, and Indonesia were the top five exporting nations. South America was the second largest exporting region, accounting for 14 per cent of the total annual value. Colombia, Brazil and Peru were the major suppliers.

Approximately 201 million fish worth $44.7 million were imported into the United States in 1992. These fish comprised 1,539 different species; 730 freshwater species, and 809 saltwater species. Freshwater fish accounted for approximately 96 per cent of the total volume and 80 per cent of the total import value. Only 32 species had import values over $10,000. The top species were freshwater and accounted for 58 per cent of the total imported value. The top imported species are the guppy, neon tetra, platy, betta, Chinese algae eater, and goldfish. Given 91.9 million total U.S. households in 1990, 9.7 million are fishkeepers. 8.8 fish per household implies a total aquarium fish population of approximately 85.7 million, suggesting that the US aquarium fish population turns over more than 2.3 times per year, counting only imported fish.

Historically, fish and plants for the first modern aquaria were gathered from the wild and transported (usually by ship) to Europea and America. During the early 20th century many species of small colourful tropical fish were exported from Manaus, Brazil; Bangkok, Thailand; Jakarta, Indonesia; the Netherlands Antilles; Kolkata, India; and other tropical countries. Import of wild fish, plants, and invertebrates for aquaria continues today around the world. Many species have not been successfully bred in captivity. In many developing countries, locals survive by collecting specimens for the aquarium trade., and continue to introduce new species to the market.

Fish Breeding

Fish breeding is a challenge that attracts many aquarists. While some species reproduce freely in community tanks, most require special conditions, known as spawning triggers before they will breed. The majority of fish lay eggs, known as spawning, and the juvenile fish that emerge are very small and need tiny live food or substitutes to survive. A fair number of popular aquarium fish are livebearers which produce a small number of relatively large offspring. These usually take ground flake food straight away.

Animal Welfare

A properly maintained aquarium allows fish to socialize with their own species and in many cases breed successfully. This is in marked contrast to the conditions of larger animals like cats and dogs, which are often kept alone and neutered in an environment different from what they would experience in the wild. However, fish are often maintained in inadequate conditions. Therefore they live short lives and never breed.

Inexperienced aquarists often keep too many fish in one tank, or add fish too quickly into an immature aquarium, killing many of them.This has given the hobby a bad reputation among some animal welfare groups, such as PETA, who accuse aquarists of treating aquarium fish as cheap toys to be replaced when they die.

Goldfish and bettas in particular have often been kept in small bowls or aquaria that are too small for their needs. In some cases fish have been installed in all sorts of inappropriate objects such as the all of which house live fish in unfiltered and insufficient water. The latter is sometimes marketed as a complete ecosystem because a plant is included in the neck of the vase. Some sellers claim the fish eat the plant roots. However, bettas are carnivorous and need live food or pellet foods. They cannot survive on plant roots. Another problem is that the plant sometimes blocks the betta's passage to the water surface. They are labyrinth fish, and need to breathe at the surface to avoid suffocation.

Such products are aimed at people looking for a novelty gift. Aquarists actively condemn them. Similarly, the awarding of goldfish as prizes at funfairs is traditional in many parts of the world, but has been criticized by aquarists and activists as cruel and irresponsible. The United Kingdom outlawed live-animal prizes such as goldfish in 2004.

The use of live prey to feed carnivorous fish such as piranhas also draws criticism.

Fish Modification

Modifying fish to make them more attractive as pets is increasingly controversial. Historically, artificially dyeing fish was common. Glassfish in particular were often injected with fluorescent dyes. The major British fishkeeping magazine, *Practical Fishkeeping*, has been effective in its campaign to remove these fish from the market by educating retailers and aquarists to the cruelty and health risks involved.

In 2006, *Practical Fishkeeping* published an article exposing the techniques for performing cosmetic surgery on aquarium fish, without anaesthesia, as described by Singaporean fishkeeping magazine *Fish Love Magazine*. The tail is cut off and dye is injected into the body. The piece also included the first documented evidence to demonstrate that parrot cichlids are injected with coloured dye. Hong Kong suppliers were offering a service in which fish could be tattooed with company logos or messages using a dye laser; such fishes have been sold in the U.K. under the name of Kaleidoscope gourami and Striped parrot cichlid. Some people give their fish body piercings.

Hybrid fish such as flowerhorn cichlids and parrot cichlids are highly controversial. Parrot cichlids in particular have a very unnatural shape that prevents them from swimming properly and makes it difficult for them to engage in normal feeding and social behaviors. The biggest concern with hybrids is that they may be bred with native species, making it difficult for hobbyists to identify and breed particular species. This is especially important to hobbyists who shelter species that are rare or extinct in the wild. Extreme mutations have been selected for by some breeders; some fancy goldfish varieties in particular have features that prevent the fish from swimming, seeing, or feeding properly.

Genetically modified fish such as the GloFish are likely to become increasingly available, particularly in the United States and Asia. Although GloFish are said to be unharmed by their genetic modifications, they remain illegal in many places, including the European Union, though at least some have been smuggled into the E.U., most likely from Taiwan, via the Czech Republic.

Conservation

The two main sources of fish for aquaria are from capture in the wild or captive breeding. United Nations studies show that more than 90 per cent of freshwater aquarium fish are captive—bred, while virtually all marine fish and invertebrates are caught. The few marine species bred in captivity supplement but rarely replace the trade in wild-caught specimens. Wild-caught animals provide valuable income for people in regions lacking other high-value exports.

Marine fish are typically less resilient during transport than freshwater fish, and relatively large numbers of them die before they reach the aquarist. Although the aquarium trade probably represents a minor threat to coral reefs compared to habitat destruction, fishing for food, and climate change, it is a booming trade and may be a serious problem in specific locations such as the Philippines and Indonesia where most collecting is done. Catching fish in the wild can reduce their population sizes, placing them in danger of extinction in collecting areas, as has been observed with the dragonet *Synchiropus splendidus*.

Collecting

In theory, reef fish should be a good example of a renewable resource that encourages fishermen to maintain the integrity and diversity of the natural habitat: more and better fish can be exported from pristine habitats than those that have been polluted or over-harvested. However, this has not been the case in similar industries such as fur trapping, logging, or fishing that experience the *tragedy of the commons*.

Fish are caught by net, trap, or cyanide. Collecting expeditions can be lengthy and costly, and are not always successful. Fish can also be injured during collection and/or shipping; mortality rates during shipping are high. Many others are weakened by stress and become diseased.

Other problems include the poisoning of coral reefs and non-target species, the depletion of rare species from their natural habitat, and ecosystem degradation from large scale removal of key species. Additionally, destructive fishing techniques concern environmentalists and hobbyists alike. There has been a concerted movement to captive breeding and certification programs for wild-caught fish. Two thirds of American marine aquarists surveyed in 1997 preferred farmed coral, and over 80 per cent think that only sustainably caught or farmed fish should be traded.

Cyanide

Cyanide is a poison that stuns and immobilizes fish. Fishers put cyanide in the ocean, to ease the process of netting them. It can irreversibly damage or kill the target fish, as well as other fish, mammals, reptiles or invertebrates that are left behind. Some U.K.-based wholesalers advertise that they avoid cyanide-caught animals. In the Philippines, overfishing and cyanide caused a drastic decline in aquarium fish, leading the country away from cyanide and towards netting healthy animals. Cyanide is also often used for collecting freshwater species, especially in muddy water with lots of vegetation, which complicates catching small and fast moving fish.

Captive Breeding and Aquaculture

Since the Siamese fighting fish (*Betta splendens*) was first successfully bred in France in 1893, captive spawning and brooding techniques used in aquaculture have slowly improved. Captive breeding for aquaria is concentrated in southern Florida, Singapore, Hong Kong and Bangkok, with smaller industries in Hawaii and Sri Lanka. Captive breeding of marine organisms has been in development since the mid-1990s. Breeding for freshwater species is more advanced than for saltwater species. Currently, only a few captive-bred marine species are in the trade, including clownfish, damselfish, and dwarf angelfish.

Aquaculture can help in lessening the impacts on wild stocks, either by using cultivated organisms for sale or by releasing them to replenish wild stocks. Breeding programs help preserve species that have become rare or extinct in the wild, most notably the Lake Victoria cichlids.

Some species have also become important as laboratory animals. Cichlids and poecilids are especially important for studies on learning, mating, and social behavior. Hobbyists also keep and observe many fishes not otherwise studied, and thereby provide valuable ecological and behavioral data.

Captive breeding has reduced prices for hobbyists, but cultured animals remain more expensive. Selective breeding has also led to wider intra–species variation, creating more diverse commercial stocks.

Invasive Species

Serious problems can occur when fish originally raised in ponds or aquaria are released into the wild. While tropical fish do not survive in temperate climates, they can thrive in waters that are similar to their native habitat. Non-native species that become established are called exotic species. Freshwater examples include various cichlids in Florida, goldfish in temperate waters, and South American suckermouth catfishes in warm waters around the world. Invasive species can seriously disrupt their new homes by preying on, or competing with, native species. Many marine fish have also been introduced into non-native waters, disrupting the local habitat.

Humane Treatment

In January 2011 the Maui County Council just passed measure requiring the aquarium fishery to adopt humane practices for preparing fish for transport to market. The regulations control harvesting and shipping practices, including prohibiting clipping the fins on fish to protect the plastic shipping bags, outlawing puncturing swim bladders that fish use to regulate their buoyancy, which enabled divers to rapidly surface and prohibiting "starving" the fish which permitted smaller shipping bags without killing the fish with their own waste. The measure also requires that shippers file mortality reports on the animals they ship.

CHAPTER

7

Aquarium

An aquarium (plural *aquariums* or *aquaria*) is a vivarium consisting of at least one transparent side in which water-dwelling plants or animals are kept. Fishkeepers use aquaria to keep fish, invertebrates, amphibians, marine mammals, turtles, and aquatic plants. The term combines the Latin root *aqua*, meaning water, with the suffix *-arium*, meaning "a place for relating to".

An aquarist owns fish or maintains an aquarium, typically constructed of glass or high strength acrylic plastic. Cuboid aquaria are also known as fish tanks or simply tanks, while bowl-shaped aquaria are also known as fish bowls. Size can range from a small glass bowl to immense public aquaria. Specialized equipment maintains appropriate water quality and other characteristics suitable for the aquarium's residents.

In the Roman Empire, the first fish to be brought indoors was the sea barbel, which was kept under guest beds in small tanks made of marble. Introduction of glass panes around the year 50 allowed Romans to replace one wall of marble tanks, improving their view of the fish. In 1369, the Chinese

Emperor, Hóngwu, established a porcelain company that produced large porcelain tubs for maintaining goldfish; over time, people produced tubs that approached the shape of modern fish bowls. Leonhard Baldner, who wrote *Vogel-, Fisch- und Tierbuch* (Bird, Fish, and Animal Book) in 1666, maintained weather loaches and newts.

In 1836, soon after his invention of the Wardian case, Ward proposed to use his tanks for tropical animals. In 1841 he did so, though only with aquatic plants and toy fish. However, he soon housed real animals. In 1838, Félix Dujardin noted owning a saltwater aquarium, though he did not use the term. In 1846, Anna Thynne maintained stony corals and seaweed for almost three years, and was credited as the creator of the first balanced marine aquarium in London. At about the same time, Robert Warington experimented with a 13-gallon container, which contained goldfish, eelgrass, and snails, creating one of the first stable aquaria. He published his findings in 1850 in the Chemical Society's journal.

The keeping of fish in an aquarium became a popular hobby and spread quickly. In the United Kingdom, it became popular after ornate aquaria in cast iron frames were featured at the Great Exhibition of 1851. In 1853, the first large public aquarium opened in the London Zoo and came to be known as the Fish House. Philip Henry Gosse was the first person to actually use the word "aquarium", opting for this term (instead of "aquatic vivarium" or "aqua-vivarium") in 1854 in his book *The Aquarium: An Unveiling of the Wonders of the Deep Sea*. In this book, Gosse primarily discussed saltwater aquaria. In the 1850s, the aquarium became a fad in the United Kingdom. Tank designs and techniques for maintaining water quality were developed by Warington, later coöperating with Gosse until his critical review of the tank water composition. Edward Edwards developed these glass-fronted aquaria in his 1858 patent for a "dark-water-chamber slope-back tank", with water slowly circulating to a reservoir beneath.

Germans soon rivaled the British in their interest. In 1854, an anonymous author had two articles published about the saltwater aquaria of the United Kingdom: *Die Gartenlaube* (The Garden House) entitled *Der Ocean auf dem Tische* (The Ocean on the Table). However, in 1856, *Der See im Glase* (The Lake in a Glass) was published, discussing freshwater aquaria, which were much easier to maintain in landlocked areas. During the 1870s, some of the first aquarist societies were appearing in Germany. The United States soon followed. Published in 1858, Henry D. Butler's *The Family Aquarium* was one of the first books written in the United States solely about the aquarium. According to the July issue of *The North American Review* of the same year, William Stimson may have owned some of the first functional aquaria, and had as many as seven or eight. The first aquarist society in the United States was founded in New York City in 1893, followed by others. The *New York Aquarium Journal*, first published in October 1876, is considered to be the world's first aquarium magazine.

In the Victorian era in the United Kingdom, a common design for the home aquarium was a glass front with the other sides made of wood (made watertight with a pitch coating). The bottom would be made of slate and heated from below. More advanced systems soon began to be introduced, along with tanks of glass in metal frames. During the latter half of the 19th century, a variety of aquarium designs were explored, such as hanging the aquarium on a wall, mounting it as part of a window, or even combining it with a birdcage.

Circa 1908, the first mechanical aquarium air pump was invented, powered by running water, instead of electricity. The introduction of the air pump into the hobby is considered by several historians of the hobby to be a pivotal moment in the development of the hobby.

Aquaria became more widely popular as houses had an electricity supply after World War I. Electricity allowed artificial lighting as well as aeration, filtration, and heating of the water. Initially, amateur aquarists kept native fish (with the exception of goldfish); the availability of exotic species from overseas further increased the popularity of the aquarium. Jugs made from a variety of materials were used to import fish from overseas, with a bicycle foot pump for aeration. Plastic shipping bags were introduced in the 1950s, making it easier to ship fish. The eventual availability of air freight allowed fish to be successfully imported from distant regions. In the 1960s metal frames made marine aquaria almost impossible due to corrosion, but the development of tar and silicone sealant allowed the first all-glass aquaria made by Martin Horowitz in Los Angeles, CA. The frames remained, however, though purely for aesthetic reasons.

In the United States, aquarium keeping is the second-most popular hobby after stamp collecting. In 1999 it was estimated that over nine million U.S. households own an aquarium. Figures from the 2005/2006 APPMA National Pet Owners Survey report that Americans own approximately 139 million freshwater fish and 9.6 million saltwater fish. Estimates of the numbers of fish kept in aquaria in Germany suggest at least 36 million. The hobby has the strongest following in Europe, Asia, and North America. In the United States, 40 per cent of aquarists maintain two or more tanks.

Most aquaria consist of glass panes bonded together by silicone, with plastic frames that are attached to the upper and lower edges for decoration. The glass aquarium is standard for sizes up to about 1000 litres (250 gal). However, glass as a material is brittle and has very little give before fracturing, though generally the sealant fails first. Aquaria come in a variety of shapes such as cuboid, hexagonal, angled to fit in a corner (L-shaped), and bow-front (the front side curves outwards). Fish bowls are generally either made of plastic or glass, and are either spherical or some other round configuration in shape.

The very first modern aquarium made of glass was developed in the 19th century by Robert Warrington. During the Victorian age it was common for glass aquaria to have slate or steel bottoms, which allow the aquaria to be heated underneath with an open flame heat source. The aquaria back then had the glass panels attached with metal frames and sealed with putty. These metal framed aquaria were still available on the market until the mid 1960s when the modern, silicone-sealed style displaced them. Acrylic tanks were not generally available to the public until the 1970s.

Although glass aquaria are usually preferred by aquarists over the acrylic ones because of their resistance to scratching and much more accessible price, they come with several disadvantages. Not only are they not as crack resistant as acrylic tanks but they are also nearly two times heavier than the latter. They also provide less insulation than acrylic aquaria and do not come in as many interesting shapes as these do. Many aquarists or beginners who want to get fish as pets find it particularly onerous that many online suppliers will not ship glass aquaria because of the high potential for cracking and the high weight, which increases the cost of shipping. However, glass tanks are more convenient for other aquarists because unlike acrylic, glass does not yellow over time, and also because glass tanks do not need as much support as acrylic aquaria.

Even though the price is one of the main aspects which is taken under consideration by aquarists when willing to purchase one of these two types of aquaria, when it comes to very large tanks the price difference tends to disappear.

Acrylic aquaria are also available and are the primary competitor with glass. Acrylic aquaria are stronger than glass, and much lighter. Acrylic-soluble cements are used to directly fuse acrylic together (as opposed to simply sealing the seam). Acrylic allows for the formation of unusual shapes, such as the hexagonal tank. Compared to glass, acrylics are easy to scratch; but unlike glass, it is possible to polish out scratches in acrylic.

Laminated glass is sometimes used, which combines the advantages of both glass and acrylic.

Large aquaria might instead use stronger materials such as fiberglass-reinforced plastics. However, this material is not transparent. Reinforced concrete is used for aquaria where weight and space are not factors. Concrete must be coated with a waterproof layer to prevent the water from breaking down the concrete as well as prevent contamination from the concrete.

Styles

Aquaria have been fashioned into coffee tables, sinks, and even toilets. Another such example is the MacQuarium, an aquarium made from the shell of an Apple Macintosh computer. In recent years, elaborate custom-designed home aquariums costing hundreds of thousands of dollars have become status symbols—according to *The New York Times*, "among people of means, a dazzling aquarium is one of the last surefire ways to impress their peers."

A kreisel tank is a circular aquarium designed to hold delicate animals such as jellyfish. These aquariums provide slow, circular water flow with a bare minimum of interior hardware, to prevent delicate animals from becoming injured by pumps or the tank itself. Originally a German design (*kreisel* means spinning top), the tank has no sharp corners, and keeps the housed animals away from the plumbing. Water moving into the tank gives a gentle flow that keeps the inhabitants suspended, and water leaving the tank is covered by a delicate screen that prevents the inhabitants from getting stuck. There are several types of kreisel tanks. In a true kreisel, a circular tank has a circular, submerged lid. Pseudokreisels have a curved bottom surface and a flat top surface, similar to the shape of either a "U" or a semicircle. Stretch kreisels or Langmuir kreisels are a "double gyre" kreisel design, where the tank length is at least twice the height. Using two downwelling inlets on both sides of the tank lets gravity create two gyres in the tank. A single downwelling inlet may be used in the middle as well. The top of a stretch kreisel may be open or closed with a lid. There may also be screens about midway down the sides of the tank, or at the top on the sides. It is possible to combine these designs; a circular shaped tank is used without a lid or cover, and the surface of the water acts as the continuation of circular flow. It is now possible to start a jellyfish aquarium at home as easily as a regular fish tank.

Another popular setup is the biotope aquarium. A biotope aquarium is a recreation of a specific natural environment. Some of the most popular biotopes (to name only a few) are the Amazon river, Rio Negro River, Lake Malawi, Lake Tanganyika, and Lake Victoria. The fish, plants, substrate, rocks, wood, and any other component of the display should match that of the natural environment. It can be a real challenge to recreate such environments and most "true" biotopes will only have a few species of fish (if not only one) and invertebrates.

An aquarium can range from a small glass bowl containing less than a litre (34 fl.oz.) of water to immense public aquaria that house entire ecosystems such as kelp forests. Relatively large home aquaria resist rapid fluctuations of temperature and pH, allowing for greater system stability.

Unfiltered bowl-shaped aquaria are now widely regarded as unsuitable for most fish. Advanced alternatives are now available. Aquariums should contain three forms of filtration: biological, mechanical and chemical to keep water conditions at suitable levels.

Reef aquaria under 100 litres (20 gal) have a special place in the aquarium hobby; these aquaria, termed nano reefs (when used in reefkeeping), have a small water volume.

Practical limitations, most notably·the weight (one litre of fresh water has a mass of 1 kilogram (8.3 lb gal^{-1}), and salt water is even denser) and internal water pressure (requiring thick glass siding) of a large aquarium, keep most home aquaria to a maximum of around 1 cubic metre in volume (1,000 kg or 2,200 lb). Some aquarists, however, have constructed aquaria of many thousands of litres.

Public aquaria designed for exhibition of large species or environments can be dramatically larger than any home aquarium. The Georgia Aquarium, for example, features an individual aquarium of 8,100,000 US gallons (30,700 m^3).

The typical hobbyist aquarium includes a filtration system, an artificial lighting system, and a heater or chiller depending on the aquarium's inhabitants. Many aquaria incorporate a hood, to decrease evaporation and prevent fish from leaving the aquarium (and anything else from entering the aquarium). They also often hold lights.

Combined biological and mechanical aquarium filtration systems are common. These either convert ammonia to nitrate (removing nitrogen at the expense of aquatic plants), or to sometimes remove phosphate. Filter media can house microbes that mediate nitrification. Filtration systems are the most complex component of home aquaria.

Aquarium heaters combine a heating element with a thermostat, allowing the aquarist to regulate water temperature at a level above that of the surrounding air, whereas coolers and chillers (refrigeration devices) are for use anywhere, such as cold water aquaria, that the ambient room temperature is above the desired tank temperature. Thermometers used include glass alcohol thermometers, adhesive external plastic strip thermometers, and battery-powered LCD thermometers. In addition, some aquarists use air pumps attached to airstones or water pumps to increase water circulation and supply adequate gas exchange at the water surface. Wave-making devices have also been constructed to provide wave action.

An aquarium's physical characteristics form another aspect of aquarium design. Size, lighting conditions, density of floating and rooted plants, placement of bog-wood, creation of caves or overhangs, type of substrate, and other factors (including an aquarium's positioning within a room) can all affect the behavior and survival of tank inhabitants.

An aquarium can be placed on an aquarium stand. Because of the weight of the aquarium, a stand must be strong as well as level. A tank that is not level may distort, leak, or crack.

These are often built with cabinets to allow storage, available in many styles to match room decor. Simple metal tank stands are also available. Most aquaria should be placed on polystyrene to cushion any irregularities on the underlying surface or the bottom of the tank itself. However, some tanks have an underframe making this unnecessary.

Large volumes of water enable more stability in a tank by diluting effects from death or contamination events that push an aquarium away from equilibrium. The bigger the tank, the easier such a systemic shock is to absorb, because the effects of that event are diluted. For example, the death of the only fish in a three U.S. gallon tank (11 L) causes dramatic changes in the system, while the death of that same fish in a 100 U.S. gallon (400 L) tank with many other fish in it represents only a minor change. For this reason, hobbyists often favor larger tanks, as they require less attention.

Several nutrient cycles are important in the aquarium. Dissolved oxygen enters the system at the surface water-air interface or via an air pump. Carbon dioxide escapes the system into the air. The phosphate cycle is an important, although often overlooked, nutrient cycle. Sulfur, iron, and micronutrients also cycle through the system, entering as food and exiting as waste. Appropriate handling of the nitrogen cycle, along with supplying an adequately balanced food supply and considered biological loading, is enough to keep these other nutrient cycles in approximate equilibrium.

An aquarium must be maintained regularly to ensure that the fish are kept healthy. Daily maintenance consists of checking the fish for signs of stress and disease, on a daily basis. Also, aquarists must make sure that the water has a good quality and it is not cloudy or foamy and the temperature of the water is appropriate for the particular species of fish that live in the aquarium.

Typical weekly maintenance includes changing around 20 per cent of the water while cleaning the gravel, or other substrate if the aquarium has one. A good habit is to replace the water extracted while "vacuuming" the gravel as this will eliminate uneaten foods and other residues that settle on the substrate. Tap water is not considered to be safe for fish to live in because it contains chemicals that harm the fish, so any tap water used must be treated with a suitable water conditioner, such as a product which removes chlorine and chloramine, and neutralises any heavy metals present. The water parameters must be checked both in the tank and in the replacing water, to make sure they are suitable for the species of fish kept.

The solute content of water is perhaps the most important aspect of water conditions, as total dissolved solids and other constituents dramatically impact basic water chemistry, and therefore how organisms interact with their environment. Salt content, or salinity, is the most basic measure of water conditions. An aquarium may have freshwater (salinity below 500 parts per million), simulating a lake or river environment; brackish water (a salt level of 500 to 30,000 PPM), simulating environments lying between fresh and salt, such as estuaries; and salt water or seawater (a salt level of 30,000 to 40,000 PPM), simulating an ocean environment. Rarely, higher salt concentrations are maintained in specialized tanks for raising brine organisms.

Saltwater is typically alkaline, while the pH (alkalinity or acidicity) of fresh water varies more. Hardness measures overall dissolved mineral content; hard or soft water may be preferred. Hard water is usually alkaline, while soft water is usually neutral to acidic. Dissolved organic content and dissolved gases content are also important factors.

Home aquarists typically use tap water supplied through their local water supply network to fill their tanks. Straight tap water cannot be used in countries that pipe chlorinated water. In the past, it was possible to "condition" the water by simply letting the water stand for a day or two, which allows the chlorine time to dissipate. However, chloramine is now used more often and does not leave the water as readily.

Additives formulated to remove chlorine or chloramine are often all that is needed to make the water ready for aquarium use. Brackish or saltwater aquaria require the addition of a commercially available mixture of salts and other minerals.

More sophisticated aquarists modify water's alkalinity, hardness, or dissolved content of organics and gases, before adding it to their aquaria. This can be accomplished by additives, such as sodium bicarbonate, to raise pH. Some aquarists filter or purify their water through deionization or reverse osmosis prior to using it. In contrast, public aquaria with large water needs often locate themselves near a natural water source (such as a river, lake, or ocean) to reduce the level of treatment.

Water temperature determines the two most basic aquarium classifications: tropical vs. cold water. Most fish and plant species tolerate only a limited temperature range: Tropical aquaria, with an average temperature of about 25 °C (77 °F), are much more common. Cold water aquaria are for fish that are better suited to a cooler environment. More important than the range is consistency; most organisms are not accustomed to sudden changes in temperatures, which can cause shock and lead to disease. Water temperature can be regulated with a thermostat and heater (or cooler).

Water movement can also be important in simulating a natural ecosystem. Aquarists may prefer anything from still water up to swift currents, depending on the aquarium's inhabitants. Water movement can be controlled via aeration from air pumps, powerheads, and careful design of internal water flow (such as location of filtration system points of inflow and outflow). Nitrogen cycle.

Of primary concern to the aquarist is management of the waste produced by an aquarium's inhabitants. Fish, invertebrates, fungi, and some bacteria excrete nitrogen waste in the form of ammonia (which converts to ammonium, in acidic water) and must then pass through the nitrogen cycle. Ammonia is also produced through the decomposition of plant and animal matter, including fecal matter and other detritus. Nitrogen waste products become toxic to fish and other aquarium inhabitants at high concentrations.

A well-balanced tank contains organisms that are able to metabolize the waste products of other aquarium residents. This process is known in the aquarium hobby as the nitrogen cycle. Bacteria known as nitrifiers (genus *Nitrosomonas*) metabolize nitrogen waste. Nitrifying bacteria capture ammonia from the water and metabolize it to produce nitrite. Nitrite is toxic to fish in high concentrations. Another type of bacteria, genus *Nitrospira*, converts nitrite into nitrate, a less toxic substance. (*Nitrobacter* bacteria were previously believed to fill this role. While biologically they could theoretically fill the same niche as Nitrospira, it has recently been found that *Nitrobacter* are not present in detectable levels in established aquaria, while *Nitrospira* are plentiful.) Commercial products sold as kits to "jump start" the nitrogen cycle, often still contain Nitrobacter.

In addition to bacteria, aquatic plants also eliminate nitrogen waste by metabolizing ammonia and nitrate. When plants metabolize nitrogen compounds, they remove nitrogen from the water by using it to build biomass that decays more slowly than ammonia-driven plankton already dissolved in the water.

Maintaining the Nitrogen Cycle

What hobbyists call the nitrogen cycle is only a portion of the complete cycle: nitrogen must be added to the system (usually through food provided to the tank inhabitants), and nitrates accumulate in the water at the end of the process, or become bound in the biomass of plants. The aquarium keeper must remove water once nitrate concentrations grow, or remove plants which have grown from the nitrates.

Hobbyist aquaria often do not have sufficient bacteria populations to adequately denitrify waste. This problem is most often addressed through two filtration solutions: Activated carbon filters absorb nitrogen compounds and other toxins, while biological filters provide a medium designed to enhance bacterial colonization. Activated carbon and other substances, such as ammonia absorbing resins, stop working when their pores fill, so these components have to be replaced regularly.

New aquaria often have problems associated with the nitrogen cycle due to insufficient beneficial bacteria. Therefore fresh water has to be matured before stocking them with fish. There are three basic approaches to this: the "fishless cycle", the "silent cycle" and "slow growth".

In a fishless cycle, small amounts of ammonia are added to an unpopulated tank to feed the bacteria. During this process, ammonia, nitrite, and nitrate levels are tested to monitor progress. The "silent" cycle is basically nothing more than densely stocking the aquarium with fast-growing aquatic plants and relying on them to consume the nitrogen, allowing the necessary bacterial populations time to develop. According to anecdotal reports, the plants can consume nitrogenous waste so efficiently that ammonia and nitrite level spikes seen in more traditional cycling methods are greatly reduced or disappear. "Slow growth" entails slowly increasing the population of fish over a period of 6 to 8 weeks, giving bacteria colonies time to grow and stabilize with the increase in fish waste.

The largest bacterial populations are found in the filter; efficient filtration is vital. Sometimes, a vigorous cleaning of the filter is enough to seriously disturb the biological balance of an aquarium. Therefore, it is recommended to rinse mechanical filters in an outside bucket of aquarium water to dislodge organic materials that contribute to nitrate problems, while preserving bacteria populations. Another safe practice consists of cleaning only half of the filter media during each service.

Aquarium Supplies

A way to keep the aquarium clean and fresh is by using specific aquarium cleaning supplies. These may include cleaning agents especially designed to clean the water and keep it fresh, nets, algae magnets and scrapers, algae pads, brushes, gravel cleaners, sealant and tongs and grabbers. A properly cleaned aquarium means healthy and happy fish. Aquarium cleaning must be performed on a regular basis to ensure that the fish are healthy. Also, by maintaining a clean aquarium one makes sure the tank looks appealing to the visitors.

Nets are very important cleaning supplies because they are helpful in transferring the fish to breeders or refugiums or to take them out of the aquarium whenever a thorough cleaning is needed. Nets come in a variety of sizes and designs. The size one needs depends on the size of the tank they need to clean.

The cleaning liquid agents are substances especially designed to clean the water without harming the health of the fish. Cleaning agents also include scratch removers, lime dissolvers, glass and acrylic polishers, wipes, salt creep removers and magnetic cleaners. All of these are intended to be used on the tank, ornaments and equipment.

Aquarium pest control products may be needed for cleaning aquaria with corals or live rocks. Aquarium pest control is helpful in fighting infestations with different organism coming from new fish or from the plants, corals or rocks that are recently acquired. If not taken care of, infestations like this may cause damage to the aquarium by depleting resources and causing illness.

The water cleaners are amongst the first aquarium cleaning supplies that must be purchased. Aquarium water conditioners and additives like chlorine removers and stress relievers make tap water safe for use in aquariums, and should be used when preparing for tank setup or water changes. The "new tank syndrome" may be avoided if using cycle aids to establish the nitrogen cycle. Also, creating the natural water conditions for an aquarium implies getting aquarium salt, vitamins and supplements.

The level of ammonia in the water must be closely monitored as a too high level of ammonia in the water may cause the death of the fish. The market provides especially designed ammonia removers which transform ammonia into a non-toxic form until the filter is able to process it. Aquarists are recommended to have ammonia removers around for immediate use in case of ammonia emergency.

Water clarifiers are used to clean up the water that might get foamy or cloudy due to chemicals or biological blooms. Overfeeding or fish death can lead to a sudden increase in organic waste which may result in biological clouding. Water clarifiers are useful in these cases. However, they should not be needed too often because excessive clouding can mean that the filters or filter media are not working properly and should be changed.

Excessive algae and cyanobacteria can be removed with the help of algaecides. Although algaecides are the fastest way to solve problems caused by algae they are not recommended in reefs, planted tanks or in those with crustaceans or livebearers. Algaecides are also not a long term solution for this type of issue and aquarists are advised to avoid direct sunlight or lights that are not intended for aquariums on their tanks because they cause algae blooms.

The cleaning supplies that are fluid such as the water purifiers or conditioners are not to replace the thorough cleaning that should be performed at least once in two weeks. However, they are handy supplies to keep the fish healthy until the aquarist can find the right time to perform such a cleaning.

Biological load is a measure of the burden placed on the aquarium ecosystem by its inhabitants. High biological loading presents a more complicated tank ecology, which in turn means that equilibrium is easier to upset. Several fundamental constraints on biological loading depend on aquarium size. The water's surface area limits oxygen intake. The bacteria population depends on the physical space they have available to colonize. Physically, only a limited size and number of plants and animals can fit into an aquarium while still providing room for movement. Biologically, biological loading refers to the rate of biological decay in proportion to tank volume.

Calculating Capacity

Limiting factors include the oxygen availability and filtration processing. Aquarists have rules of thumb to estimate the number of fish that can be kept in an aquarium. The examples below are for small freshwater fish; larger freshwater fishes and most marine fishes need much more generous allowances.

- 3 cm of *adult* fish length per 4 litres of water (i.e., a 6 cm-long fish would need about 8 litres of water).
- cm of *adult* fish length per 30 square centimetres of surface area.
- 1 inch of *adult* fish length per gallon of water.
- 1 inch of *adult* fish length per 12 square inches of surface area.

Experienced aquarists warn against applying these rules too strictly because they do not consider other important issues such as growth rate, activity level, social behaviour, surface area of plant life, and so on. Establishing maximum capacity is often a matter of slowly adding fish and monitoring water quality over time, following a trial and error approach.

Other Factors Affecting Capacity

One variable is differences between fish. Smaller fish consume more oxygen per gram of body weight than larger fish. Labyrinth fish can breathe atmospheric oxygen and do not need as much surface area (however, some of these fish are territorial, and do not appreciate crowding). Barbs also require more surface area than tetras of comparable size.

Oxygen exchange at the surface is an important constraint, and thus the surface area of the aquarium matters. Some aquarists claim that a deeper aquarium holds no more fish than a shallower aquarium with the same surface area. The capacity can be improved by surface movement and water circulation such as through aeration, which not only improves oxygen exchange, but also waste decomposition rates.

Waste density is another variable. Decomposition in solution consumes oxygen. Oxygen dissolves less readily in warmer water; this is a double-edged sword since warmer temperatures make fish more active, so they consume more oxygen.

In addition to bioload/chemical considerations, aquarists also consider the mutual compatibility of the fish. For instance, predatory fish are usually not kept with small, passive species, and territorial fish are often unsuitable tankmates for shoaling species. Furthermore, fish tend to fare better if given tanks conducive to their size. That is, large fish need large tanks and small fish can do well in smaller tanks. Lastly, the tank can become overcrowded without being overstocked. In other words, the aquarium can be suitable with regard to filtration capacity, oxygen load, and water, yet still be so crowded that the inhabitants are uncomfortable.

General Aquarium Description (Freshwater)

Identifying care methods that work for all aquarists is extremely difficult as there are several maintenance routines frequently used that have proven successful for keeping aquarium fish. However, there have been some studies done on freshwater aquarium systems that do indicate successfult trends in aquarium care. According to one study in particular that polled data from one hundred freshwater aquarists, the median/average conditions of the freshwater aquarium were described as follows:

- Median Tank Size: 37 Gallons (inconclusive)
- Median Stocking Density: 13 Fish at 2 Inches Each (more being worse with regard to lethality but not necessarily efficiency)
- Median Water Change Frequency: 7 Days (inconclusive, no trend)

- Median Water Change percentage: 30 per cent (very large water changes may be detrimental to efficiency, but not lethality)
- Median Lighting Wattage: 40 Watts (more watts being better)
- Median Plantedness: Moderately Planted (more plants being better if appropriately cared for)
- Average Snail Presence: 53 per cent (snails seem to be associated with better efficiency and lower lethality)
- Average Fertilizer Presence: 48 per cent (fertilizers seem to function like snails)
- Best Overall Filter Type: Canister (hang-on-back filters are the most prevalent, worst filter type with regard to lethality while hang-on-back with additional bio-filtration filters are the most prevalent, worst filters with regard to efficiency).

The above list represents the midpoints of freshwater aquarium dynamics, meaning that freshwater aquariums that are close to these parameters are likely to be at least moderately successful. Nonetheless, the study did confirm that some extreme parameter configurations were successful despite not being close to these parameters.

From the outdoor ponds and glass jars of antiquity, modern aquaria have evolved into a wide range of specialized systems. Individual aquaria can vary in size from a small bowl large enough for only a single small fish, to the huge public aquaria that can simulate entire marine ecosystems.

One way to classify aquaria is by salinity. Freshwater aquaria are the most popular due to their lower cost.

More expensive and complex equipment is required to set up and maintain a marine aquaria. Marine aquaria frequently feature a diverse range of invertebrates in addition to species of fish. Brackish water aquaria combine elements of both marine and freshwater fishkeeping. Fish kept in brackish water aquaria generally come from habitats with varying salinity, such as mangroves and estuaries. Subtypes exist within these types, such as the reef aquarium, a typically smaller marine aquarium that houses coral.

Another classification is by temperature range. Many aquarists choose a tropical aquarium because tropical fish tend to be more colorful. However, the coldwater aquarium is also popular, which is mainly restricted to goldfish, but can include fish from temperate areas worldwide and native fish keeping.

Aquaria may be grouped by their species selection. The community tank is the most common today, where several non-aggressive species live peacefully. In these aquaria, the fish, invertebrates, and plants probably do not originate from the same geographic region, but tolerate similar water conditions. Aggressive tanks, in contrast, house a limited number of species that can be aggressive toward other fish, or are able to withstand aggression well. Most marine tanks and tanks housing Cichlids have to take the aggressiveness of the desired species into account when stocking. Specimen tanks usually only house one fish species, along with plants, perhaps found in the fishes' natural environment and decorations simulating a natural ecosystem. This type is useful for fish that cannot coexist with other fish, such as the electric eel, as an extreme example. Some tanks of this sort are used simply to house adults for breeding.

Ecotype, ecotope, or biotope aquaria is another type based on species selection. In it, an aquarist attempts to simulate a specific natural ecosystem, assembling fish, invertebrate species, plants, decorations and water conditions all found in that ecosystem. These biotope aquaria are the most sophisticated hobby aquaria; public aquaria use this approach whenever possible. This approach best simulates the experience of observing in the wild. It typically serves as the healthiest possible artificial environment for the tank's occupants.

Most public aquarium facilities feature a number of smaller aquaria, as well those too large for home aquarists. The largest tanks hold millions of gallons of water and can house large species, including sharks or beluga whales. Dolphinaria are specifically for dolphins. Aquatic and semiaquatic animals, including otters and penguins, may also be kept by public aquaria. Public aquaria may also be included in larger establishments such as a marine mammal park or a marine park.

Virtual Aquariums

A virtual aquarium is a computer program which uses 3D graphics to reproduce an aquarium on a personal computer. The swimming fish are rendered in real time, while the background of the tank is usually static. Objects on the floor of the tank may be mapped in simple planes so that the fish may appear to swim both in front and behind them, but a relatively simple 3D map of the general shape of such objects may be used to allow the light and ripples on the surface of the water to cast realistic shadows. Bubbles and water noises are common for virtual aquariums, which are often used as screensavers.

The number of each type of fish can usually be selected, often including other animals like starfish, jellyfish, seahorses, and even sea turtles. Most companies that produce virtual aquarium software also offer other types of fish for sale via Internet download. Other objects found in an aquarium can also be added and rearranged on some software, like treasure chests and giant clams that open and close with air bubbles, or a bobbing diver. There are also usually features that allow the user to tap on the glass or put food in the top, both of which the fish will react to. Some also have the ability to allow the user to edit fish and other objects to create new varieties.

CHAPTER

8

The Science of Fish

A fish is any gill-bearing aquatic vertebrate (or craniate) animal that lacks limbs with digits. Included in this definition are the living hagfish, lampreys, and cartilaginous and bony fish, as well as various extinct related groups. Because the term is defined negatively, and excludes the tetrapods (i.e., the amphibians, reptiles, birds and mammals) which descend from within the same ancestry, it is paraphyletic. The traditional term pisces (also ichthyes) is considered a typological, but not a phylogenetic classification.

Most fish are "cold-blooded", or ectothermic, allowing their body temperatures to vary as ambient temperatures change. Fish are abundant in most bodies of water. They can be found in nearly all aquatic environments, from high mountain streams (e.g., char and gudgeon) to the abyssal and even hadal depths of the deepest oceans (e.g., gulpers and anglerfish). At 31,900 species, fish exhibit greater species diversity than any other class of vertebrates.

Fish, especially as food, are an important resource worldwide. Commercial and subsistence fishers hunt fish in wild fisheries (see fishing) or farm them in ponds or in cages in the ocean (see aquaculture). They are also caught by recreational fishers, kept as pets, raised by fishkeepers, and exhibited in public aquaria. Fish have had a role in culture through the ages, serving as deities, religious symbols, and as the subjects of art, books and movies.

The term "fish" most precisely describes any non-tetrapod craniate (i.e. an animal with a skull and in most cases a backbone) that has gills throughout life and whose limbs, if any, are in the shape of fins. Unlike groupings such as birds or mammals, fish are not a single clade but a paraphyletic collection of taxa, including hagfishes, lampreys, sharks and rays, ray-finned fish, coelacanths, and lungfish. Indeed, lungfish and coelacanths are closer relatives of tetrapods (such as mammals, birds, amphibians, etc.) than of other fish such as ray-finned fish or sharks, so the last common ancestor of all fish is also an ancestor to tetrapods. As paraphyletic groups are no longer recognised in modern systematic biology, the use of the term "fish" as a biological group must be avoided.

Many types of aquatic animals commonly referred to as "fish" are not fish in the sense given above; examples include shellfish, cuttlefish, starfish, crayfish and jellyfish. In earlier times, even biologists did not make a distinction – sixteenth century natural historians classified also seals, whales, amphibians, crocodiles, even hippopotamuses, as well as a host of aquatic invertebrates, as fish. However, according the definition above, all mammals, including Cetaceans like Whales and Dolphins, are not fish. In some contexts, especially in aquaculture, the true fish are referred to as finfish (or fin fish) to distinguish them from these other animals.

A typical fish is ectothermic, has a streamlined body for rapid swimming, extracts oxygen from water using gills or uses an accessory breathing organ to breathe atmospheric oxygen, has two sets of paired fins, usually one or two (rarely three) dorsal fins, an anal fin, and a tail fin, has jaws, has skin that is usually covered with scales, and lays eggs.

Some palaeontologists contend that because Conodonta are chordates, they are primitive fish. For a fuller treatment of this taxonomy, see the vertebrate article.

The position of hagfish in the phylum chordata is not settled. Phylogenetic research in 1998 and 1999 supported the idea that the hagfish and the lampreys form a natural group, the Cyclostomata, that is a sister group of the Gnathostomata.

The various fish groups account for more than half of vertebrate species. There are almost 28,000 known extant species, of which almost 27,000 are bony fish, with 970 sharks, rays, and chimeras and about 108 hagfish and lampreys. A third of these species fall within the nine largest families; from largest to smallest, these families are Cyprinidae, Gobiidae, Cichlidae, Characidae, Loricariidae, Balitoridae, Serranidae, Labridae, and Scorpaenidae. About 64 families are monotypic, containing only one species. The final total of extant species may grow to exceed 32,500.

Each criterion has exceptions. Tuna, swordfish, and some species of sharks show some warm-blooded adaptations—they can heat their bodies significantly above ambient water temperature. Streamlining and swimming performance varies from fish such as tuna, salmon, and jacks that can cover 10-20 body-lengths per second to species such as eels and rays that swim no more than 0.5 body-lengths per second. Many groups of freshwater fish extract oxygen from the air as well as from the water using a variety of different structures. Lungfish have paired lungs similar to those of tetrapods, gouramis have a structure called the labyrinth organ that performs a similar function, while many catfish, such as *Corydoras* extract oxygen via the intestine or stomach. Body shape and the arrangement of the fins is highly variable, covering such seemingly unfishlike forms as seahorses, pufferfish, anglerfish, and gulpers. Similarly, the surface of the skin may be naked (as in moray eels), or covered with scales of a variety of different types usually defined as placoid (typical of sharks and rays), cosmoid (fossil lungfish and coelacanths), ganoid (various fossil fish but also living gars and bichirs), cycloid, and ctenoid (these last two are found on most bony fish). There are even fish that live mostly on land. Mudskippers feed and interact with one another on mudflats and go underwater to hide in their burrows. The catfish *Phreatobius cisternarum* lives in underground; phreatic habitats, and a relative lives in waterlogged leaf litter.

Most fish exchange gases using gills on either side of the pharynx. Gills consist of threadlike structures called filaments. Each filament contains a capillary network that provides a large surface area for exchanging oxygen and carbon dioxide. Fish exchange gases by pulling oxygen-rich water through their mouths and pumping it over their gills. In some fish, capillary blood flows in the opposite direction to the water, causing counter current exchange. The gills push the oxygen-poor water out through openings in the sides of the pharynx. Some fish, like sharks and lampreys, possess multiple gill openings. However, most fish have a single gill opening on each side. This opening is hidden beneath a protective bony cover called an operculum.

Many fish can breathe air via a variety of mechanisms. The skin of anguillid eels may absorb oxygen. The buccal cavity of the electric eel may breathe air. Catfish of the families Loricariidae, Callichthyidae, and Scoloplacidae absorb air through their digestive tracts. Lungfish, with the exception of the Australian lungfish, and bichirs have paired lungs similar to those of tetrapods and must surface to gulp fresh air through the mouth and pass spent air out through the gills. Gar and bowfin have a vascularized swim bladder that functions in the same way. Loaches, trahiras, and many catfish breathe by passing air through the gut. Mudskippers breathe by absorbing oxygen across the skin (similar to frogs). A number of fish have evolved so-called accessory breathing organs that extract oxygen from the air. Labyrinth fish (such as gouramis and bettas) have a labyrinth organ above the gills that performs this function. A few other fish have structures resembling labyrinth organs in form and function, most notably snakeheads, pikeheads, and the Clariidae catfish family.

Breathing air is primarily of use to fish that inhabit shallow, seasonally variable waters where the water's oxygen concentration may seasonally decline. Fish dependent solely on dissolved oxygen, such as perch and cichlids, quickly suffocate, while air-breathers survive for much longer, in some cases in water that is little more than wet mud. At the most extreme, some air-breathing fish are able to survive in damp burrows for weeks without water, entering a state of aestivation (summertime hibernation) until water returns.

Fish can be divided into obligate air breathers and facultative air breathers. Obligate air breathers, such as the African lungfish, *must* breathe air periodically or they suffocate. Facultative air breathers, such as the catfish *Hypostomus plecostomus*, only breathe air if they need to and will otherwise rely on their gills for oxygen. Most air breathing fish are facultative air breathers that avoid the energetic cost of rising to the surface and the fitness cost of exposure to surface predators.

Circulation

Fish have a closed-loop circulatory system. The heart pumps the blood in a single loop throughout the body. In most fish, the heart consists of four parts, including two chambers and an entrance and exit. The first part is the sinus venosus, a thin-walled sac that collects blood from the fish's veins before allowing it to flow to the second part, the atrium, which is a large muscular chamber. The atrium serves as a one-way antechamber, sends blood to the third part, ventricle. The ventricle is another thick-walled, muscular chamber and it pumps the blood, first to the fourth part, bulbous arteriosus, a large tube, and then out of the heart. The bulbus arteriosus connects to the aorta, through which blood flows to the gills for oxygenation.

Digestion

Jaws allow fish to eat a wide variety of food, including plants and other organisms. Fish ingest food through the mouth and break it down in the esophagus. In the stomach, food is further digested and, in many fish, processed in finger-shaped pouches called pyloric caeca, which secrete digestive enzymes and absorb nutrients. Organs such as the liver and pancreas add enzymes and various chemicals as the food moves through the digestive tract. The intestine completes the process of digestion and nutrient absorption.

Excretion

As with many aquatic animals, most fish release their nitrogenous wastes as ammonia. Some of the wastes diffuse through the gills. Blood wastes are filtered by the kidneys.

Saltwater fish tend to lose water because of osmosis. Their kidneys return water to the body. The reverse happens in freshwater fish: they tend to gain water osmotically. Their kidneys produce dilute urine for excretion. Some fish have specially adapted kidneys that vary in function, allowing them to move from freshwater to saltwater.

Scales

The scales of fish originate from the mesoderm (skin); they may be similar in structure to teeth.

SENSORY AND NERVOUS SYSTEM

Central Nervous System

Fish typically have quite small brains relative to body size compared with other vertebrates, typically one-fifteenth the brain mass of a similarly sized bird or mammal. However, some fish have relatively large brains, most notably mormyrids and sharks, which have brains about as massive relative to body weight as birds and marsupials.

Fish brains are divided into several regions. At the front are the olfactory lobes, a pair of structures that receive and process signals from the nostrils via the two olfactory nerves. The olfactory lobes are very large in fish that hunt primarily by smell, such as hagfish, sharks, and catfish. Behind the olfactory lobes is the two-lobed telencephalon, the structural equivalent to the cerebrum in higher vertebrates. In fish the telencephalon is concerned mostly with olfaction. Together these structures form the forebrain.

Connecting the forebrain to the midbrain is the diencephalon (in the diagram, this structure is below the optic lobes and consequently not visible). The diencephalon performs functions associated with hormones and homeostasis. The pineal body lies just above the diencephalon. This structure detects light, maintains circadian rhythms, and controls color changes.

The midbrain or mesencephalon contains the two optic lobes. These are very large in species that hunt by sight, such as rainbow trout and cichlids.

The hindbrain or metencephalon is particularly involved in swimming and balance. The cerebellum is a single-lobed structure that is typically the biggest part of the brain. Hagfish and lampreys have relatively small cerebellae, while the mormyrid cerebellum is massive and apparently involved in their electrical sense.

The brain stem or myelencephalon is the brain's posterior. As well as controlling some muscles and body organs, in bony fish at least, the brain stem governs respiration and osmoregulation.

Sense Organs

Most fish possess highly developed sense organs. Nearly all daylight fish have color vision that is at least as good as a human's. Many fish also have chemoreceptors that are responsible for extraordinary senses of taste and smell. Although they have ears, many fish may not hear very well. Most fish have sensitive receptors that form the lateral line system, which detects gentle currents and vibrations, and senses the motion of nearby fish and prey. Some fish, such as catfish and sharks, have organs that detect low-level electric current. Other fish, like the electric eel, can produce electric current.

Fish orient themselves using landmarks and may use mental maps based on multiple landmarks or symbols. Fish behavior in mazes reveals that they possess spatial memory and visual discrimination.

Capacity for Pain

Experiments done by William Tavolga provide evidence that fish have pain and fear responses. For instance, in Tavolga's experiments, toadfish grunted when electrically shocked and over time they came to grunt at the mere sight of an electrode.

In 2003, Scottish scientists at the University of Edinburgh and the Roslin Institute concluded that rainbow trout exhibit behaviors often associated with pain in other animals. Bee venom and acetic acid injected into the lips resulted in fish rocking their bodies and rubbing their lips along the sides and floors of their tanks, which the researchers concluded were attempts to relieve pain, similar to what mammals would do. Neurons fired in a pattern resembling human neuronal patterns.

Professor James D. Rose of the University of Wyoming claimed the study was flawed since it did not provide proof that fish possess "conscious awareness, particularly a kind of awareness that is meaningfully like ours". Rose argues that since fish brains are so different from human brains, fish are probably not conscious in the manner humans are, so that reactions similar to human reactions to pain instead have other causes. Rose had published a study a year earlier arguing that fish cannot feel pain because their brains lack a neocortex. However, animal behaviorist Temple Grandin argues that fish could still have consciousness without a neocortex because "different species can use different brain structures and systems to handle the same functions."

Animal welfare advocates raise concerns about the possible suffering of fish caused by angling. Some countries, such as Germany have banned specific types of fishing, and the British RSPCA now formally prosecutes individuals who are cruel to fish.

Most fish move by alternately contracting paired sets of muscles on either side of the backbone. These contractions form S-shaped curves that move down the body. As each curve reaches the back fin, backward force is applied to the water, and in conjunction with the fins, moves the fish forward. The fish's fins function like an airplane's flaps. Fins also increase the tail's surface area, increasing speed. The streamlined body of the fish decreases the amount of friction from the water. Since body tissue is denser than water, fish must compensate for the difference or they will sink. Many bony fish have an internal organ called a swim bladder that adjusts their buoyancy through manipulation of gases.

Homeothermy

Although most fish are exclusively aquatic and ectothermic, there are exceptions to both cases.

Fish from multiple groups can live out of the water for extended time periods. Amphibious fish such as the mudskipper can live and move about on land for up to several days.

Certain species of fish maintain elevated body temperatures. Endothermic teleosts (bony fish) are all in the suborder Scombroidei and include the billfishes, tunas, and one species of "primitive" mackerel (*Gasterochisma melampus*). All sharks in the family Lamnidae – shortfin mako, long fin mako, white, porbeagle, and salmon shark – are endothermic, and evidence suggests the trait exists in family Alopiidae (thresher sharks). The degree of endothermy varies from the billfish, which warm only their eyes and brain, to bluefin tuna and porbeagle sharks who maintain body temperatures elevated in excess of 20°C above ambient water temperatures. Endothermy, though metabolically costly, is thought to provide advantages such as increased muscle strength, higher rates of central nervous system processing, and higher rates of digestion.

Fish reproductive organs include testes and ovaries. In most species, gonads are paired organs of similar size, which can be partially or totally fused. There may also be a range of secondary organs that increase reproductive fitness.

In terms of spermatogonia distribution, the structure of teleosts testes has two types: in the most common, spermatogonia occur all along the seminiferous tubules, while in Atherinomorph fish they are confined to the distal portion of these structures. Fish can present cystic or semi-cystic spermatogenesis in relation to the release phase of germ cells in cysts to the seminiferous tubules lumen.

Fish ovaries may be of three types: gymnovarian, secondary gymnovarian or cystovarian. In the first type, the oocytes are released directly into the coelomic cavity and then enter the ostium, then through the oviduct and are eliminated. Secondary gymnovarian ovaries shed ova into the coelom from which they go directly into the oviduct. In the third type, the oocytes are conveyed to the exterior through the oviduct. Gymnovaries are the primitive condition found in lungfish, sturgeon, and bowfin. Cystovaries characterize most teleosts, where the ovary lumen has continuity with the oviduct. Secondary gymnovaries are found in salmonids and a few other teleosts.

Oogonia development in teleosts fish varies according to the group, and the determination of oogenesis dynamics allows the understanding of maturation and fertilization processes. Changes in the nucleus, ooplasm, and the surrounding layers characterize the oocyte maturation process.

Postovulatory follicles are structures formed after oocyte release; they do not have endocrine function, present a wide irregular lumen, and are rapidly reabsorbed in a process involving the apoptosis of follicular cells. A degenerative process called follicular atresia reabsorbs vitellogenic oocytes not spawned. This process can also occur, but less frequently, in oocytes in other development stages.

Some fish are hermaphrodites, having both testes and ovaries either at different phases in their life cycle or, as in hamlets, have them simultaneously.

Reproductive Method

Over 97 per cent of all known fish are oviparous, that is, the eggs develop outside the mother's body. Examples of oviparous fish include salmon, goldfish, cichlids, tuna, and eels. In the majority of these species, fertilisation takes place outside the mother's body, with the male and female fish shedding their gametes into the surrounding water. However, a few oviparous fish practice internal fertilization, with the male using some sort of intromittent organ to deliver sperm into the genital opening of the female, most notably the oviparous sharks, such as the horn shark, and oviparous rays, such as skates. In these cases, the male is equipped with a pair of modified pelvic fins known as claspers.

Marine fish can produce high numbers of eggs which are often released into the open water column. The eggs have an average diameter of The newly hatched young of oviparous fish are called larvae. They are usually poorly formed, carry a large yolk sac (for nourishment) and are very different in appearance from juvenile and adult specimens. The larval period in oviparous fish is relatively short (usually only several weeks), and larvae rapidly grow and change appearance and structure (a process termed metamorphosis) to become juveniles. During this transition larvae must switch from their yolk sac to feeding on zooplankton prey, a process which depends on typically inadequate zooplankton density, starving many larvae.

In ovoviviparous fish the eggs develop inside the mother's body after internal fertilization but receive little or no nourishment directly from the mother, depending instead on the yolk. Each embryo develops in its own egg. Familiar examples of ovoviviparous fish include guppies, angel sharks, and coelacanths.

Some species of fish are viviparous. In such species the mother retains the eggs and nourishes the embryos. Typically, viviparous fish have a structure analogous to the placenta seen in mammals connecting the mother's blood supply with that of the embryo. Examples of viviparous fish include the surf-perches, splitfins, and lemon shark. Some viviparous fish exhibit oophagy, in which the developing embryos eat other eggs produced by the mother. This has been observed primarily among sharks, such as the shortfin mako and porbeagle, but is known for a few bony fish as well, such as the halfbeak *Nomorhamphus ebrardtii*. Intrauterine cannibalism is an even more unusual mode of vivipary, in which the largest embryos eat weaker and smaller siblings. This behavior is also most commonly found among sharks, such as the grey nurse shark, but has also been reported for *Nomorhamphus ebrardtii*.

Immune System

Immune organs vary by type of fish. In the jawless fish (lampreys and hagfish), true lymphoid organs are absent. These fish rely on regions of lymphoid tissue within other organs to produce immune cells. For example, erythrocytes, macrophages and plasma cells are produced in the anterior kidney (or pronephros) and some areas of the gut (where granulocytes mature.) They resemble primitive bone marrow in hagfish. Cartilaginous fish (sharks and rays) have a more advanced immune system. They have three specialized organs that are unique to chondrichthyes; the epigonal organs (lymphoid tissue similar to mammalian bone) that surround the gonads, the Leydig's organ within the walls of their esophagus, and a spiral valve in their intestine. These organs house typical immune cells (granulocytes, lymphocytes and plasma cells). They also possess an identifiable thymus and a well-developed spleen (their most important immune organ) where various lymphocytes, plasma cells and macrophages develop and are stored. Chondrostean fish (sturgeons, paddlefish and bichirs) possess a major site for the production of granulocytes within a mass that is associated with the meninges (membranes surrounding the central nervous system.) Their heart is frequently covered with tissue that contains lymphocytes, reticular cells and a small number of macrophages. The chondrostean kidney is an important hemopoietic organ; where erythrocytes, granulocytes, lymphocytes and macrophages develop.

Like chondrostean fish, the major immune tissues of bony fish (or teleostei) include the kidney (especially the anterior kidney), which houses many different immune cells. In addition, teleost fish possess a thymus, spleen and scattered immune areas within mucosal tissues (e.g. in the skin, gills, gut and gonads). Much like the mammalian immune system, teleost erythrocytes, neutrophils and granulocytes are believed to reside in the spleen whereas lymphocytes are the major cell type found in the thymus. In 2006, a lymphatic system similar to that in mammals was described in one species of teleost fish, the zebrafish. Although not confirmed as yet, this system presumably will be where naive (unstimulated) T cells accumulate while waiting to encounter an antigen.

Like other animals, fish suffer from diseases and parasites. To prevent disease they have a variety of defenses. *Non-specific* defences include the skin and scales, as well as the mucus layer secreted by the epidermis that traps and inhibits the growth of micro-organisms. If pathogens breach these defenses, fish can develop an inflammatory response that increases blood flow to the infected region and delivers white blood cells that attempt to destroy pathogens. Specific defenses respond to particular pathogens recognised by the fish's body, i.e., an immune response. In recent years, vaccines have become widely used in aquaculture and also with ornamental fish, for example furunculosis vaccines in farmed salmon and koi herpes virus in koi.

Some species use cleaner fish to remove external parasites. The best known of these are the Bluestreak cleaner wrasses of the genus *Labroides* found on coral reefs in the Indian and Pacific Oceans. These small fish maintain so-called "cleaning stations" where other fish congregate and perform specific movements to attract the attention of the cleaners. Cleaning behaviors have been observed in a number of fish groups, including an interesting case between two cichlids of the same genus, *Etroplus maculatus*, the cleaner, and the much larger *Etroplus suratensis*. Fish do not represent a monophyletic group, and therefore the "evolution of fish" is not studied as a single event.

Proliferation of fish was apparently due to the hinged jaw, because jawless fish left very few descendants. Lampreys may approximate pre-jawed fish. The first jaws are found in Placodermi fossils. It is unclear if the advantage of a hinged jaw is greater biting force, improved respiration, or a combination of factors.

Fish may have evolved from a creature similar to a coral-like Sea squirt, whose larvae resemble primitive fish in important ways. The first ancestors of fish may have kept the larval form into adulthood (as some sea squirts do today), although perhaps the reverse is the case.

The 2006 IUCN Red List names 1173 fish species that are threatened with extinction. Included are species such as Atlantic cod, Devil's Hole pupfish, coelacanths, and great white sharks. Because fish live underwater they are more difficult to study than terrestrial animals and plants, and information about fish populations is often lacking. However, freshwater fish seem particularly threatened because they often live in relatively small water bodies. For example, the Devil's Hole pupfish occupies only a single 3 by 6 metres (10 by 20 ft) pool.

Overfishing

Overfishing is a major threat to edible fish such as cod and tuna. Overfishing eventually causes population (known as stock) collapse because the survivors cannot produce enough young to replace those removed. Such commercial extinction does not mean that the species is extinct, merely that it can no longer sustain a fishery.

One well-studied example of fishery collapse is the Pacific sardine *Sadinops sagax caerulues* fishery off the California coast. From a 1937 peak of 790,000 long tons (800,000 t) the catch steadily declined to only 24,000 long tons (24,000 t) in 1968, after which the fishery was no longer economically viable.

The main tension between fisheries science and the fishing industry is that the two groups have different views on the resiliency of fisheries to intensive fishing. In places such as Scotland, Newfoundland, and Alaska the fishing industry is a major employer, so governments are predisposed to support it. On the other hand, scientists and conservationists push for stringent protection, warning that many stocks could be wiped out within fifty years.

Habitat Destruction

A key stress on both freshwater and marine ecosystems is habitat degradation including water pollution, the building of dams, removal of water for use by humans, and the introduction of exotic species. An example of a fish that has become endangered because of habitat change is the pallid sturgeon, a North American freshwater fish that lives in rivers damaged by human activity.

Exotic Species

Introduction of non-native species has occurred in many habitats. One of the best studied examples is the introduction of Nile perch into Lake Victoria in the 1960s. Nile perch gradually exterminated the lake's 500 endemic cichlid species. Some of them survive now in captive breeding programmes, but others are probably extinct. Carp, snakeheads, tilapia, European perch, brown trout, rainbow trout, and sea lampreys are other examples of fish that have caused problems by being introduced into a lien environments.

Aquarium Collecting Culture

Among the deities said to take the form of a fish are Ika-Roa of the Polynesians, Dagon of various ancient Semitic peoples, the shark-gods of Hawaii and *Matsya* of the Dravidas of India. The astrological symbol Pisces is based on a constellation of the same name, but there is also a second fish constellation in the night sky, Piscis Austrinus.

Fish have been used figuratively in many different ways, for example the ichthys used by early Christians to identify themselves, through to the fish as a symbol of fertility among Bengalis.

Fish feature prominently in art and literature, in movies such as *Finding Nemo* and books such as *The Old Man and the Sea*. Large fish, particularly sharks, have frequently been the subject of horror movies and thrillers, most notably the novel *Jaws*, which spawned a series of films of the same name that in turn inspired similar films or parodies such as *Shark Tale*, *Snakehead Terror*, and *Piranha*.

In the semiotic of *Ashtamangala* (buddhist symbolism) the golden fish (Sanskrit: *Matsya*), represents the state of fearless suspension in *samsara*, perceived as the harmless ocean, referred to as 'Buddha-eyes' or *'rigpa-sight'*. The fish symbolizes the auspiciousness of all living beings in a state of fearlessness without danger of drowning in the Samsaric Ocean of Suffering, and migrating from teaching to teaching freely and spontaneously just as fish swim.

They have religious significance in Hindu, Jain and Buddhist traditions but also in Christianity who is first signified by the sign of the fish, and especially referring to feeding the multitude in the desert. In the dhamma of Buddha the fish symbolize happiness as they have complete freedom of movement in the water. They represent fertility and abundance. Often drawn in the form of carp which are regarded in the Orient as sacred on account of their elegant beauty, size and life-span.

The name of the Canadian city of Coquitlam, British Columbia is derived from *Kwikwetlem*, which is said to be derived from a Coast Salish term meaning "little red fish".

A random assemblage of fish merely using some localised resource such as food or nesting sites is known simply as an *aggregation*. When fish come together in an interactive, social grouping, then they may be forming either a *shoal* or a *school* depending on the degree of organisation. A *shoal* is a loosely organised group where each fish swims and forages independently but is attracted to other members of the group and adjusts its behaviour, such as swimming speed, so that it remains close to the other members of the group. *Schools* of fish are much more tightly organised, synchronising their swimming so that all fish move at the same speed and in the same direction. Shoaling and schooling behaviour is believed to provide a variety of advantages.

Examples:

- Cichlids congregating at lekking sites form an *aggregation*.
- Many minnows and characins form *shoals*.
- Anchovies, herrings and silversides are classic examples of *schooling* fish.

While school and shoal have different meanings within biology, they are often treated as synonyms by non-specialists, with speakers of British English using "shoal" to describe any grouping of fish, while speakers of American English often using "school" just as loosely.

CHAPTER 9

Technology of Wild Fisheries

A fishery is an area with an associated fish or aquatic population which is harvested for its commercial value. Fisheries can be marine (saltwater) or freshwater. They can also be wild or farmed. This article is an overview of the habitats occupied by the worlds' wild fisheries, and the human impacts on those habitats.

Wild fisheries are sometimes called capture fisheries. The aquatic life they support is not controlled in any meaningful way and needs to be "captured" or fished. Wild fisheries exist primarily in the oceans, and particularly around coasts and continental shelves. They also exist in lakes and rivers. Issues with wild fisheries are overfishing and pollution. Significant wild fisheries have collapsed or are in danger of collapsing, due to overfishing and pollution. Overall, production from the world's wild fisheries has levelled out, and may be starting to decline.

As a contrast to wild fisheries, farmed fisheries can operate in sheltered coastal waters, in rivers, lakes and ponds, or in enclosed bodies of water such as tanks. Farmed fisheries are technological in nature, and revolve around developments in aquaculture. Farmed fisheries are expanding, and Chinese aquaculture in particular is making many advances. Nevertheless, the majority of fish consumed by humans continues to be sourced from wild fisheries. As of the early 21st century, fish is humanity's only significant wild food source.

According to the Food and Agriculture Organization (FAO), the world harvest by commercial fisheries in 2005 consisted of 93.2 million tonnes of aquatic animals captured in wild fisheries, plus another 1.3 million tons of aquatic plants (seaweed etc). This can be contrasted with 48.1 million tonnes harvested in fish farms and 14.8 million tons of aquatic plants produced by aquaculture.

An ocean current is continuous, directed movement of ocean water. Ocean currents are rivers of relatively warm or cold water within the ocean. The currents are generated from the forces acting upon the water like the planet rotation, the wind, the temperature and salinity (hence isopycnal) differences and the gravitation of the moon. The depth contours, the shoreline and other currents influence the current's direction and strength.

Gyres and Upwelling

Oceanic gyres are large-scale ocean currents caused by the Coriolis effect. Wind-driven surface currents interact with these gyres and the underwater topography, such as seamounts and the edge of continental shelves, to produce downwellings and upwellings. These can transport nutrients and provide feeding grounds for plankton eating forage fish. This in turn draws larger fish that predate on the forage fish, and can result in productive fishing grounds. Most upwellings are coastal, and many of them support some of the most productive fisheries in the world, such as small pelagics (sardines, anchovies, etc.). Regions of upwelling include coastal Peru, Chile, Arabian Sea, western South Africa, eastern New Zealand and the California coast. In the ocean, the food chain typically follows the course:

- Phytoplankton
- Zooplankton
- Predatory zooplankton filter feeders
- Predatory fish

Phytoplankton is usually the primary producer (the first level in the food chain or the first trophic level). Phytoplankton converts inorganic carbon into protoplasm. Phytoplankton is consumed by microscopic animals called zooplankton. These are the second level in the food chain, and include krill, the larva of fish, squid, lobsters and crabs–as well as the small crustaceans called copepods, and many other types. Zooplankton is consumed both by other, larger predatory zooplankters and by fish (the third level in the food chain). Fish that eat zooplankton could constitute the fourth trophic level, while seals consuming the fish are the fifth. Alternatively, for example, whales may consume zooplankton directly - leading to an environment with one less trophic level. Aquatic habitats have been classified into marine and freshwater ecoregions by the Worldwide Fund for Nature (WWF). An ecoregion is defined as a "relatively large unit of land or water containing a characteristic set of natural communities that share a large majority of their species, dynamics, and environmental conditions.

Coastal Waters

Estuaries are semi-enclosed coastal bodies of water with one or more rivers or streams flowing into therm, and with a free connection to the open sea. Estuaries are often associated with high rates of biological productivity. They are small, in demand, impacted by events far upstream or out at sea, and concentrate materials such as pollutants and sediments. Lagoons are bodies of comparatively shallow salt or brackish water separated from the deeper sea by a shallow or exposed sandbank, coral reef, or similar feature. *Lagoon* refers to both coastal lagoons formed by the build-up of sandbanks or reefs along shallow coastal waters, and the lagoons in atolls, formed by the growth of coral reefs on slowly sinking central islands. Lagoons that are fed by freshwater streams are estuaries.

The intertidal zone (foreshore) is the area that is exposed to the air at low tide and submerged at high tide, for example, the area between tide marks. This area can include many different types of habitats, including steep rocky cliffs, sandy beaches or vast mudflats. The area can be a narrow strip, as in Pacific islands that have only a narrow tidal range, or can include many meters of shoreline where shallow beach slope interacts with high tidal excursion.

Fixed-net fishing on the littoral zone along the Suhua Highway on the East coast of Taiwan.

The littoral zone is the part of the ocean closest to the shore. The word *littoral* comes from the Latin *litoralis*, which means *seashore*. The littoral zone extends from the high water mark to near shore areas that are permanently submerged, and includes the intertidal zone. Definitions vary. Encyclopaedia Britannica defines the littoral zone in a thoroughly vague way as the "marine ecological realm that experiences the effects of tidal and longshore currents and breaking waves to a depth of 5 to 10 metres (16 to 33 feet) below the low-tide level, depending on the intensity of storm waves". The US Navy defines it as extending "from the shoreline to 600 feet (183 meters) out into the water".

The sublittoral zone is the part of the ocean extending from the seaward edge of the littoral zone to the edge of the continental shelf. It is sometimes called the neritic zone. Websters defines the neritic zone as the region of shallow water adjoining the seacoast. The word *neritic* perhaps comes from the new Latin *nerita*, which refers to a genus of marine snails, 1891. The sublittoral zone is relatively shallow, extending to about 200 meters (100 fathoms), and generally has well-oxygenated water, low water pressure, and relatively stable temperature and salinity levels. These, combined with presence of light and the resulting photosynthetic life, such as phytoplankton and floating sargassum, make the sublittoral zone the location of the majority of sea life.

Continental shelves are the extended perimeters of each continent and associated coastal plain, which is covered during interglacial periods such as the current epoch by relatively shallow seas (known as shelf seas) and gulfs.

The shelf usually ends at a point of decreasing slope (called the shelf break). The sea floor below the break is the continental slope. Below the slope is the continental rise, which finally merges into the deep ocean floor, the abyssal plain. The continental shelf and the slope are part of the continental margin.

Continental shelves are shallow (averaging 140 metres or 460 feet), and the sunlight available means they can teem with life. The shallowest parts of the continental shelf are called fishing banks. There the sunlight penetrates to the seafloor and the plankton, on which fish feed, thrive.

Coral reefs are aragonite structures produced by living organisms, found in shallow, tropical marine waters with little to no nutrients in the water. High nutrient levels such as those found in runoff from agricultural areas can harm the reef by encouraging the growth of algae. Although corals are found both in temperate and tropical waters, reefs are formed only in a zone extending at most from 30°N to 30°S of the equator.

In the deep ocean, much of the ocean floor is a flat, featureless underwater desert called the abyssal plain. Many pelagic fish migrate across these pains in search of spawning or different feeding grounds. Smaller migratory fish are followed by larger predator fish and can provide rich, if temporary, fishing grounds. A seamount is an underwater mountain, rising from the seafloor that does not reach to the water's surface (sea level), and thus is not an island. They are defined by oceanographers as independent features that rise to at least 1,000 meters above the seafloor. Seamounts are common in the Pacific Ocean. Past studies suggest there may be 30,000 seamounts in the Pacific, about 1000 in the Atlantic Ocean and an unknown number in the Indian Ocean.

Freshwater Fisheries Lakes

Worldwide, freshwater lakes have an area of 1.5 million square kilometres. Saline inland seas add another 1.0 million square kilometres. There are 28 freshwater lakes with an area greater than 5,000 square kilometres, totalling 1.18 million square kilometres or 79 per cent of the total.

Rivers Pollution

Pollution is the introduction of contaminants into an environment. Wild fisheries flourish in oceans, lakes, and rivers, and the introduction of contaminants is an issue of concern, especially as regards plastics, pesticides, heavy metals, and other industrial and agricultural pollutants which do not disintegrate rapidly in the environment. Land run-off and industrial, agricultural, and domestic waste enter rivers and are discharged into the sea. Pollution from ships is also a problem.

Plastic Waste

Marine debris is human-created waste that ends up floating in the sea. Oceanic debris tends to accumulate at the centre of gyres and coastlines, frequently washing aground where it is known as beach litter. Eighty per cent of all known marine debris is plastic - a component that has been rapidly accumulating since the end of World War II. Plastics accumulate because they don't biodegrade as many other substances do; while they will photodegrade on exposure to the sun, they do so only under dry conditions, as water inhibits this process.

Discarded plastic bags, six pack rings and other forms of plastic waste which finish up in the ocean present dangers to wildlife and fisheries. Aquatic life can be threatened through entanglement, suffocation, and ingestion.

Nurdles, also known as mermaids' tears, are plastic pellets typically under five millimetres in diameter, and are a major contributor to marine debris. They are used as a raw material in plastics manufacturing, and are thought to enter the natural environment after accidental spillages. Nurdles are also created through the physical weathering of larger plastic debris. They strongly resemble fish eggs, only instead of finding a nutritious meal, any marine wildlife that ingests them will likely starve, be poisoned and die.

Many animals that live on or in the sea consume flotsam by mistake, as it often looks similar to their natural prey. Plastic debris, when bulky or tangled, is difficult to pass, and may become permanently lodged in the digestive tracts of these animals, blocking the passage of food and causing death through starvation or infection. Tiny floating particles also resemble zooplankton, which can lead filter feeders to consume them and cause them to enter the ocean food chain. In samples taken from the North Pacific Gyre in 1999 by the Algalita Marine Research Foundation, the mass of plastic exceeded that of zooplankton by a factor of six. More recently, reports have surfaced that there may now be 30 times more plastic than plankton, the most abundant form of life in the ocean.

Toxic additives used in the manufacture of plastic materials can leech out into their surroundings when exposed to water. Waterborne hydrophobic pollutants collect and magnify on the surface of plastic debris, thus making plastic far more deadly in the ocean than it would be on land. Hydrophobic contaminants are also known to bioaccumulate in fatty tissues, biomagnifying up the food chain and putting great pressure on apex predators. Some plastic additives are known to disrupt the endocrine system when consumed, others can suppress the immune system or decrease reproductive rates.

Toxins

Apart from plastics, there are particular problems with other toxins which do not disintegrate rapidly in the marine environment. Heavy metals are metallic chemical elements that have a relatively high density and are toxic or poisonous at low concentrations. Examples are mercury, lead, nickel, arsenic and cadmium. Other persistent toxins are PCBs, DDT, pesticides, furans, dioxins and phenols.

Such toxins can accumulate in the tissues of many species of aquatic life in a process called bioaccumulation. They are also known to accumulate in benthic environments, such as estuaries and bay muds: a geological record of human activities of the last century.

Some specific examples are:

- Chinese and Russian industrial pollution such as phenols and heavy metals in the Amur River have devastated fish stocks and damaged its estuary soil.
- Wabamun Lake in Alberta, Canada, once the best whitefish lake in the area, now has unacceptable levels of heavy metals in its sediment and fish.
- Acute and chronic pollution events have been shown to impact southern California kelp forests, though the intensity of the impact seems to depend on both the nature of the contaminants and duration of exposure.
- Due to their high position in the food chain and the subsequent accumulation of heavy metals from their diet, mercury levels can be high in larger species such as bluefin and albacore. As a result, in March 2004 the United States FDA issued guidelines recommending that pregnant women, nursing mothers and children limit their intake of tuna and other types of predatory fish.
- Some shellfish and crabs can survive polluted environments, accumulating heavy metals or toxins in their tissues. For example, mitten crabs have a remarkable ability to survive in highly modified aquatic habitats, including polluted waters. The farming and harvesting of such species needs careful management if they are to be used as a food.
- Mining has a poor environmental track record. For example, according to the United States Environmental

Protection Agency, mining has contaminated portions of the headwaters of over 40 per cent of watersheds in the western continental US. Much of this pollution finishes up in the sea.

- Heavy metals enter the environment through oil spills - such as the Prestige oil spill on the Galician coast - or from other natural or anthropogenic sources.

Eutrophication

Eutrophication is an increase in chemical nutrients, typically compounds containing nitrogen or phosphorus, in an ecosystem. It can result in an increase in the ecosystem's primary productivity (excessive plant growth and decay), and further effects including lack of oxygen and severe reductions in water quality, fish, and other animal populations.

The biggest culprit are rivers that empty into the ocean, and with it the many chemicals used as fertilizers in agriculture as well as waste from livestock and humans. An excess of oxygen depleting chemicals in the water can lead to hypoxia and the creation of a dead zone.

Surveys have shown that 54 per cent of lakes in Asia are eutrophic; in Europe, 53 per cent; in North America, 48 per cent; in South America, 41 per cent; and in Africa, 28 per cent. Estuaries also tend to be naturally eutrophic because land-derived nutrients are concentrated where run-off enters the marine environment in a confined channel. The World Resources Institute has identified 375 hypoxic coastal zones around the world, concentrated in coastal areas in Western Europe, the Eastern and Southern coasts of the US, and East Asia, particularly in Japan. In the ocean, there are frequent red tide algae blooms that kill fish and marine mammals and cause respiratory problems in humans and some domestic animals when the blooms reach close to shore.

In addition to land runoff, atmospheric anthropogenic fixed nitrogen can enter the open ocean. A study in 2008 found that this could account for around one third of the ocean's external (non-recycled) nitrogen supply and up to three per cent of the annual new marine biological production. It has been suggested that accumulating reactive nitrogen in the environment may have consequences as serious as putting carbon dioxide in the atmosphere.

The oceans are normally a natural carbon sink, absorbing carbon dioxide from the atmosphere. Because the levels of atmospheric carbon dioxide are increasing, the oceans are becoming more acidic. The potential consequences of ocean acidification are not fully understood, but there are concerns that structures made of calcium carbonate may become vulnerable to dissolution, affecting corals and the ability of shellfish to form shells.

A report from NOAA scientists published in the journal Science in May 2008 found that large amounts of relatively acidified water are upwelling to within four miles of the Pacific continental shelf area of North America. This area is a critical zone where most local marine life lives or is born. While the paper dealt only with areas from Vancouver to northern California, other continental shelf areas may be experiencing similar effects.

EFFECTS OF FISHING

Habitat Destruction

Fishing nets that have been left or lost in the ocean by fishermen are called ghost nets, and can entangle fish, dolphins, sea turtles, sharks, dugongs, crocodiles, seabirds, crabs, and other creatures. Acting as designed, these nets restrict movement, causing starvation, laceration and infection, and—in those that need to return to the surface to breath—suffocation.

Overfishing

On the east coast of the United States, the availability of bay scallops has been greatly diminished by the overfishing of sharks in the area. A variety of sharks have, until recently, fed on rays, which are a main predator of bay scallops. With the shark population reduced, in some places almost totally, the rays have been free to dine on scallops to the point of greatly decreasing their numbers.

Chesapeake Bay's once-flourishing oyster populations historically filtered the estuary's entire water volume of excess nutrients every three or four days. Today that process takes almost a year, and sediment, nutrients, and algae can cause problems in local waters. Oysters filter these pollutants, and either eat them or shape them into small packets that are deposited on the bottom where they are harmless.

The Australian government alleged in 2006 that Japan illegally overfished southern bluefin tuna by taking 12,000 to 20,000 tonnes per year instead of the their agreed 6,000 tonnes; the value of such overfishing would be as much as USD $2 billion. Such overfishing has resulted in severe damage to stocks. "Japan's huge appetite for tuna will take the most sought-after stocks to the brink of commercial extinction unless fisheries agree on more rigid quotas" stated the WWF Japan disputes this figure, but acknowledges that some overfishing has occurred in the past.

Loss of Biodiversity

Each species in an ecosystem is affected by the other species in that ecosystem. There are very few single prey-single predator relationships. Most prey are consumed by more than one predator, and most predators have more than one prey. Their relationships are also influenced by other environmental factors. In most cases, if one species is removed from an ecosystem, other species will most likely be affected, up to the point of extinction.

Species biodiversity is a major contributor to the stability of ecosystems. When an organism exploits a wide range of resources, a decrease in biodiversity is less likely to have an impact. However, for an organism which exploit only limited resources, a decrease in biodiversity is more likely to have a strong effect.

Reduction of habitat, hunting and fishing of some species to extinction or near extinction, and pollution tend to tip the balance of biodiversity. For a systematic treatment of biodiversity within a trophic level, see unified neutral theory of biodiversity.

Threatened Species

The global standard for recording threatened marine species is the IUCN Red List of Threatened Species. This list is the foundation for marine conservation priorities worldwide. A species is listed in the threatened category if it is considered to be critically endangered, endangered, or vulnerable. Other categories are near threatened and data deficient.

Marine

Many marine species are under increasing risk of extinction and marine biodiversity is undergoing potentially irreversible loss due to threats such as overfishing, bycatch, climate change, invasive species and coastal development.

By 2008, the IUCN had assessed about 3,000 marine species. This includes assessments of known species of shark, ray, chimaera, reef-building coral, grouper, marine turtle, seabird, and marine mammal. Almost one-quarter (22%) of these groups have been listed as threatened .

Sharks, rays, and chimaeras: are deep water pelagic species, which makes them difficult to study in the wild. Not a lot is known about their ecology and population status. Much of what is currently known is from their capture in nets from both targeted and accidental catch. Many of these slow growing species are not recovering from overfishing by shark fisheries around the world.

Groupers: Major threats are overfishing, particularly the uncontrolled fishing of small juveniles and spawning adults.

Coral reefs: The primary threats to corals are bleaching and disease which has been linked to an increase in sea temperatures. Other threats include coastal development, coral extraction, sedimentation and pollution. The coral triangle (Indo-Malay-Philippine archipelago) region has the highest number of reef-building coral species in threatened category as well as the highest coral species diversity. The loss of coral reef ecosystems will have devastating effects on many marine species, as well as on people that depend on reef resources for their livelihoods.

Marine mammals: It include whales, dolphins, porpoises, seals, sea lions, walruses, sea otter, marine otter, manatees, dugong and the polar bear. Major threats include entanglement in ghost nets, targeted harvesting, noise pollution from military and seismic sonar, and boat strikes. Other threats are water pollution, habitat loss from coastal development, loss of food sources due to the collapse of fisheries, and climate change.

- *Seabirds:* Major threats include longline fisheries and gillnets, oil spills, and predation by rodents and cats in their breeding grounds. Other threats are habitat loss and degradation from coastal development, logging and pollution.
- *Marine turtles:* Marine turtles lay their eggs on beaches, and are subject to threats such as coastal development, sand mining, and predators, including humans who collect their eggs for food in many parts of the world. At sea, marine turtles can be targeted by small scale subsistence fisheries, or become bycatch during longline and trawling activities, or become entangled in ghost nets or struck by boats.

An ambitious project, called the Global Marine Species Assessment, is under way to make IUCN Red List assessments for another 17,000 marine species by 2012. Groups targeted include the approximately 15,000 known marine fishes, and important habitat-forming primary producers such mangroves, seagrasses, certain seaweeds and the remaining corals; and important invertebrate groups including molluscs and echinoderms.

Freshwater fisheries have a disproportionately high diversity of species compared to other ecosystems. Although freshwater habitats cover less than 1 per cent of the world's surface, they provide a home for over 25 per cent of known vertebrates, more than 126,000 known animal species, about 24,800 species of freshwater fish, molluscs, crabs and dragonflies, and about 2,600 macrophytes.

Continuing industrial and agricultural developments place huge strain on these freshwater systems. Waters are polluted or extracted at high levels, wetlands are drained, rivers channelled, forests deforestated leading to sedimentation, invasive species are introduced, and over-harvesting occurs.

In the 2008 IUCN Red List, about 6,000 or 22 per cent of the known freshwater species have been assessed at a global scale, leaving about 21,000 species still to be assessed. This makes clear that, worldwide, freshwater species are highly threatened, possibly more so than species in marine fisheries. However, a significant proportion of freshwater species are listed as data deficient, and more field surveys are needed.

Fisheries Management

A recent paper published by the National Academy of Sciences of the USA warns that: "Synergistic effects of habitat destruction, overfishing, introduced species, warming, acidification, toxins, and massive runoff of nutrients are transforming once complex ecosystems like coral reefs and kelp forests into monotonous level bottoms, transforming clear and productive coastal seas into anoxic dead zones, and transforming complex food webs topped by big animals into simplified, microbially dominated ecosystems with boom and bust cycles of toxic dinoflagellate blooms, jellyfish, and disease".

CHAPTER 10

Aquaponics

Aquaponics is a sustainable food production system that combines a traditional aquaculture (raising aquatic animals such as fish, crayfish or prawns in tanks) with hydroponics (cultivating plants in water) in a a symbiotic environment. In the aquaculture, effluents accumulate in the water, increasing toxicity for the fish. This water is led to a hydroponic system where the by-products from the aquaculture are filtered out by the plants as vital nutrients, after which the cleansed water is recirculated back to the animals. The term *aquaponics* is a portmanteau of the terms *aquaculture* and *hydroponic*.

Aquaponic systems vary in size from small indoor or outdoor units to large commercial units, using the same technology. The systems usually contain fresh water, but salt water systems are plausible depending on the type of aquatic animal and vegetation. Aquaponic science may still be considered to be at an early stage.

Aquaponics consists of two main parts with the aquaculture part for raising aquatic animals and the hydroponics part for growing plants. Aquatic effluents resulting from uneaten feed or raising animals like fish accumulates in water due to the closed system recirculation of most aquaculture systems. The effluent-rich water becomes toxic to the aquatic animal in high concentrations but these effluents are nutrients essential for plant growth. Although consisting primarily of these two parts, aquaponics system are usually grouped into several components or subsystems for the effective removal of solid wastes, the addition of bases to neutralize acids, and to maintain water oxygenation. They include the:

- *Rearing tank*: The tanks for raising and feeding the fish;
- *Solids removal*: A unit for catching uneaten food and detached biofilms, and for settling out fine particulates;
- *Biofilter*: A place where the nitrification bacteria can grow and convert ammonia into nitrates, which are usable by the plants;
- *Hydroponics subsystem*: The portion of the system where plants are grown by absorbing excess nutrients from the water;
- *Sump*: The lowest point in the system where the water flows to and from which it is pumped back to the rearing tanks.

Depending on the sophistication and cost of the aquaponics system, the units for solids removal, biofiltration, and/or the hydroponics subsystem may be combined into one unit or subsystem, which prevent the water from flowing directly from the aquaculture part of the system to the hydroponics part.

Nitrification in an aquaponics system is dependent on bacterial biofilm located in a specific biofiltering module or distributed throughout the system.

Although selected minerals or nutrients such as iron are sometimes added, the main source of nutrients for the plants is the fish waste. Ammonia is steadily released into the water through the excreta and gills of fish as a product of their metabolism. Higher concentrations of ammonia (commonly between 500 and 1,000 ppm) can kill fish, and plants do not absorb it as well as nitrates. This means that nitrification, or the aerobic conversion of toxic ammonia into nitrates, is one of the most important functions in aquaponics since it reduces the toxicity of the water and makes it easier for the plants to take up the nitrogenous compounds. By maintaining a healthy population of *Nitrosomonas* bacteria that convert ammonia into nitrites, and *Nitrobacter* bacteria that convert nitrites into nitrates, the toxicity of the water is reduced and the resulting compounds can be removed by the plants for nourishment. This process occurs throughout the system, as the bacteria responsible for this process will form a biofilm on all solid surfaces of the system in contact with the water. The submerged roots of the vegetables combined have a large surface area so that many bacteria can accumulate here. Most aquaponics systems include a biofiltering unit, which helps facilitate growth of these micro-organisms. Typically, ammonia levels range from 0.25 to 2.0 ppm; nitrite levels range from 0.25 to 1 ppm, and nitrate levels range from 2 to 150 ppm. During system startup, spikes may occur in the levels of ammonia (up to 6.0 ppm) and nitrite (up to 15 ppm), with nitrate levels peaking later in the startup phase. Since the nitrification process acidifies the water, non-sodium bases such as potassium hydroxide or calcium hydroxide can be added for neutralizing the water's pH if insufficient quantities are naturally present in the water to provide a buffer against acidification.

A good way to deal with solids buildup in aquaponics is the use of worms, which make the solid organic matter liquid so that they can be utilized by the plants or and animals.

Plants are grown with their roots immersed in the nutrient-rich effluent water similar to hydroponic systems. This enables them to utilize the nutrient-rich water and filter out the compounds toxic to the aquatic animals. After the water has passed through the hydroponic subsystem, it is clean and oxygenated and can return to the aquaculture. This cycle is continuous. Common aquaponic applications of hydroponic systems include:

- *Deep-water raft aquaponics*: styrofoam rafts floating in a relatively deep aquaculture basin in troughs.
- *Recirculating aquaponics*: solid media such as gravel or clay beads, held in a container that is flooded with water from the aquaculture. This type of aquaponics is also known as *closed-loop aquaponics*.
- *Reciprocating aquaponics*: solid media in a container that is alternately flooded and drained utilizing different types of siphon drains. This type of aquaponics is also known as *flood-and-drain aquaponics* or *ebb-and-flow aquaponics*.
- Other systems use towers that are trickle-fed from the top, nutrient film technique channels, horizontal PVC pipes with holes for the pots, plastic barrels cut in half with gravel or rafts in them. Each approach has its own benefits.

Aquaculture Subsystem

Freshwater fish are the most common aquatic animal raised using aquaponics, although saltwater fish, crayfish and prawns may also be used. In practice, tilapia are the most popular fish chosen for home and commercial projects that are intended to raise edible fish, however barramundi and Murray cod are also used. Most green leaf vegetables grow well in the hydroponic filter, although most profitable are varieties of chinese cabbage, lettuce, basil, roses, tomatoes, okra, cantaloupe and bell peppers. Other species of vegetables that grow well in an aquaponic system include beans, peas, kohlrabi, watercress, taro, radishes, strawberries, melons, onions, turnips, parsnips, and herbs. Since plants at different growth stages require different amounts of minerals and nutrients, plant harvesting is staggered with seedings growing at the same time as mature plants. This ensures stable nutrient content in the water because of continuous symbiotic cleansing of toxins from the water that in high levels kill fish.

Aquaponic systems do not typically discharge or exchange water under normal operation, but instead recirculate and reuse water very effectively. The system relies on the relationship between the animals and the plants to maintain a stable aquatic environment that experience a minimal of fluctuation in ambient nutrient and oxygen levels. Water is only added to replace water loss from absorption and transpiration by plants, evaporation into the air from surface water, overflow from the system from rainfall, and removal of biomass such as settled solid wastes from the system. As a result, aquaponics uses approximately 2 per cent of the water that a conventionally irrigated farm requires for the same vegetable production. This allows for aquaponic production of both crops and fish in areas where water or fertile land is scarce. Aquaponic systems can also be used to replicate controlled wetland conditions that are useful for water treatment by reclaiming potable water from typical household sewage. The nutrient-filled overflow water can be accumulated in catchment tank, and reused to accelerate growth of crops grown in soil, or it may be pumped back into the aquaponic system to compensate for the water lost in periods of drought or little rainfall.

The three main inputs to the system are water, feed given to the aquatic animals, and electricity to pump water between the aquaculture and the hydroponics. The hydroponics system continually provides plants such as vegetables, while the aquaculture can contain edible species of among others fish, but they will have to be replaced to keep the system stable.

Aquaponics has ancient roots, although there is some debate on its first occurrence:

- Aztec cultivated agricultural islands known as *chinampas* and are considered by some as the first form of aquaponics for agricultural use, where plants were raised on stationary islands in lake shallows and waste materials dredged from the Chinampa canals and surrounding cities are used to manuallly irrigate the plants.

At the New Alchemy Institute, researchers experimented with bioshelters and wastewater management via crop production. This pursuit, of what was to become the permaculture movement founded on the one element/many functions principle, inspired researchers to advance the concept of fish effluent as fertilizer for crop production. The institute published a series of article describing the use of fish pond water to irrigate plants. However the described techniques did not explicitly create a symbiotic and circulatory growth environment for what was to become aquaponics.

Formal scientific interest in the combining of aquaculture and hydroponics started in the mid-1970s. One of the earliest scholarly papers was written by Sneed, Allen, and Ellis. It would take another decade before a greater amount of research in the integration of the two areas would start to crystallize into the true beginnings of aquaponics. Research by aquacultural scientists introduced the solar-algae hydroponic aquaculture pond, which further promoted attention for integrating plants into a system of aquaculture.

The first known recirculating (closed-loop) and reciprocating (flood-and-drain or ebb-and-flow) aquaponic system, called the Integrated Aqua-Vegeculture System, was built by then-graduate student and his professors. It filtered tilapia effluent into sand biofilters containing bacteria, which filtered out animal waste and dead algae from the water while it provided nutrients to tomato, cucumber and other vegetable crops.

United States

Inspired by the successes of the New Alchemy Institute and the North Carolina State University with aquaponics, other institutes followed suit. Besides the reciprocating aquaponics based on the techniques developed by Dr. Mark McMurtry *et al.* at the New Alchemy Institute and North Carolina State University, Dr. James Rakocy and his colleagues at the University of the Virgin Islands researched and developed the "Deep Water" or "Raft Culture" aquaponics The system combines tilapia with various vegetables.

In 1997 Rebecca L. Nelson and John S. Pade began publishing the *Aquaponics Journal*, a quarterly scientific journal that brings together research and various applications of aquaponics from around the globe. In 2008, they wrote and published the first comprehensive book on aquaponics, *Aquaponic Food Production*. Nelson and Pade work closely with Dr. Rakocy to bring the research on aquaponics into mainstream agriculture, and offer systems, supplies, training and consultancy professionally.

Recent years have seen a shift towards community integration of aquaponics, such as the nonprofit foundation Growing Power that offers Milwaukee youth job opportunities and training while growing food for their community. The model has spawned several satellite projects in other cities. In 2010, a partnership of experts in sustainable agriculture was formed under the name AquaPlanet to promote the technology through media and consulting. The team includes Dr. Mark McMurtry, and Travis Hughey who invented Barrel-Ponics™.

Canada

The first aquaponics research in Canada was a small system added onto existing aquaculture research at a research station in Lethbridge. Canada saw a rise in aquaponics setups throughout the 90s, predominantly as commercial installations, that for example combine trout with floating lettuce production, or to water fruiting vegetable crops that warm up the water too much to be recirculated back into the fish ponds. Eels are also known to be raised. A set-up based on the deep water system developed at the University of Virgin Islands was built in a greenhouse at Brooks, Alberta where Dr. Nick Savidov and colleagues researched aquaponics from a background of plant science. The team made findings on rapid root growth in aquaponics systems, on closing the solid waste loop, and that because of certain advantages in the system over traditional aquaculture, the system can run well at a low pH level, which is favoured by plants but not fish.

The Edmonton Aquaponics Society in Northern Alberta is adapting Dr. Savidov's commercially sized system to a smaller scale prototype that can be operated by families, small groups, or restaurants. They intend to further develop the closed solid waste loop.

SOUTH AMERICA

Barbados

Barbados is a densely populated island that deals with water scarcity. In 40 years' time, focus has shifted from domestic fruit and vegetable production on small farms to importing 80 per cent of all fruits and vegetables for cost reasons. Aquaponics would make Barbados and other Caribbean islands less dependent on the world food market and reduce stress on the dwindling fish supplies. An inter-organizational project that started in late 2009 sets out to encourage and enable Barbadians to start aquaponics at home, with revenue generated by selling produce to tourists.

Australia

Due to a ban on tilapia in all states except for Western Australia, native freshwater fish including silver perch, jade perch, sleepy cod, murray cod and barramundi are popular in aquaponics and aquaculture systems, along with non-native rainbow trout, brown trout and crayfish such as yabby and redclaw.

The unique advantages of aquaponic systems are:

- Conservation through constant water reuse and recycling.
- Organic fertilization of plants with natural fish emulsion.
- The elimination of solid waste disposal from intensive aquaculture.
- The reduction of needed cropland to produce crops.
- The overall reduction of the environmental footprint of crop production.
- Building small efficient commercial installations near markets reduces food miles.

Some conceivable disadvantages with aquaponics are:

- Initial expenses for housing, tank, plumbing, pumps, and grow beds.
- The infinite number of ways in which a system can be configured lends itself to equally varying results, conflicting research, and successes or failures.

Some aquaponic installations rely heavily on man-made energy, technological solutions, and environmental control to achieve recirculation and water/ambient temperatures. However, if a system is designed with energy conservation in mind, among others using alternative energy and gravity to reduce pumping, it can be extremely energy efficient.

Whilst careful design can minimize the risk, aquaponics systems can have multiple 'single points of failure' where problems such as an electrical failure or a pipe blockage can lead to a complete loss of fish stock.

Like all aquaculture based systems, stock feed usually consists of fish meal derived from lower value species. Ongoing depletion of wild fish stocks makes this practice unsustainable. Organic fish feeds may prove to be a viable alternative that negates this concern. Other alternatives include growing duckweed with an aquaponics system that feeds the same fish grown on the system, excess worms grown from vermiculture composting, as well as growing black soldier fly larvae to feed to the fish using composting grub growers.

CHAPTER 11

Salmon

Salmon is the common name for Salmonidae. Several other fish in the family are called trout; the difference is often said to be that salmon migrate and trout are resident, a distinction that holds true for the *Salmo* genus. Salmon live along the coasts of both the North Atlantic (one migratory species *Salmo salar*) and Pacific Oceans (approximately a dozen species of the genus *Oncorhynchus*), as well as having been introduced into the Great Lakes of North America.

Typically, salmon are anadromous: they are born in fresh water, migrate to the ocean, then return to fresh water to reproduce. However, there are populations of several species that are restricted to fresh water through their life. Folklore has it that the fish return to the exact spot where they were born to spawn; tracking studies have shown this to be true, and this homing behavior has been shown to depend on olfactory memory. Salmon are intensively produced in aquaculture in many parts of the world.

Salmon eggs are laid in freshwater streams typically at high latitudes. The eggs hatch into *alevin* or *sac fry*. The fry quickly develop into *parr* with camouflaging vertical stripes. The parr stay for 6 months to three years in their natal stream before becoming *smolts*, which are distinguished by their bright silvery colour with scales that are easily rubbed off. It is estimated that only 10 per cent of all salmon eggs survive to this stage. The smolt body chemistry changes, allowing them to live in salt water. Smolts spend a portion of their out-migration time in brackish water, where their body chemistry becomes accustomed to osmoregulation in the ocean.

The salmon spend about one to five years (depending on the species) in the open ocean where they gradually become sexually mature. The adult salmon then return primarily to their natal stream to spawn. In Alaska, the crossing-over to other streams allows salmon to populate new streams, such as those that emerge as a glacier retreats. The precise method salmon use to navigate has not been established, though their keen sense of smell is involved. Atlantic salmon spend between one and four years at sea. (When a fish returns after just one year's sea feeding it is called a *grilse* in Canada, the UK and Ireland.) Prior to spawning, depending on the species, salmon undergo changes. They may grow a hump, develop canine teeth, develop a *kype* (a pronounced curvature of the jaws in male salmon). All will change from the silvery blue of a fresh run fish from the sea to a darker color. Salmon can make amazing journeys, sometimes moving hundreds of miles upstream against strong currents and rapids to reproduce. Chinook and sockeye salmon from central Idaho, for example, travel over 900 miles (1400 km) and climb nearly 7000 feet (2100 m) from the Pacific ocean as they return to spawn. Condition tends to deteriorate the longer the fish remain in fresh water, and they then deteriorate further after they spawn, when they are known as *kelts*. In all species of Pacific salmon, the mature individuals die within a few days or weeks of spawning, a trait known as semelparity. Between 2 per cent and 4 per cent of Atlantic salmon kelts survive to spawn again, all females. However, even in those species of salmon that may survive to spawn more than once (iteroparity), post-spawning mortality is quite high (perhaps as high as 40 to 50%.)

To lay her roe, the female salmon uses her tail (caudal fin), to create a low-pressure zone, lifting gravel to be swept downstream, excavating a shallow depression, called a *redd*. The redd may sometimes contain 5000 eggs covering 30 square feet (2.8 m^2). The eggs usually range from orange to red. One or more males will approach the female in her redd, depositing his sperm, or milt, over the roe. The female then covers the eggs by disturbing the gravel at the upstream edge of the depression before moving on to make another redd. The female will make as many as 7 redds before her supply of eggs is exhausted.

Each year, the fish experiences a period of rapid growth, often in summer, and one of slower growth, normally in winter. This results in rings (annuli) analogous to the growth rings visible in a tree trunk. Freshwater growth shows as densely crowded rings, sea growth as widely spaced rings; spawning is marked by significant erosion as body mass is converted into eggs and milt.

Freshwater streams and estuaries provide important habitat for many salmon species. They feed on terrestrial and aquatic insects, amphipods, and other crustaceans while young, and primarily on other fish when older. Eggs are laid in deeper water with larger gravel, and need cool water and good water flow (to supply oxygen) to the developing embryos. Mortality of salmon in the early life stages is usually high due to natural predation and human-induced changes in habitat, such as siltation, high water temperatures, low oxygen concentration, loss of stream cover, and reductions in river flow. Estuaries and their associations wetlands provide vital nursery areas for the salmon prior to their departure to the open ocean. Wetlands not only help buffer the estuary from silt and pollutants, but also provide important feeding and hiding areas.

Species

The various species of salmon have many names, and varying behaviours.

The Atlantic Ocean has only one species of salmon, in the genus *Salmo*:

- Atlantic salmon, or salmon, (*Salmo salar*) reproduce in northern rivers on both coasts of the ocean.
- Land-locked salmon (*Salmo salar* m. *sebago*) live in a number of lakes in eastern North America and in Northern Europe, for instance in lakes Onega, Ladoga, Saimaa and Vänern. They are not a different species from the Atlantic salmon, but have independently evolved a non-migratory life cycle, which they maintain even when they can access the ocean.

Pacific Ocean Species

Pacific species belong to the genus *Oncorhynchus*, some examples include:

- Cherry salmon or seema (*Oncorhynchus masou*) is found only in the western Pacific Ocean in Japan, Korea and Russia. There is also a landlocked subspecies known as the *Taiwanese salmon* or *Formosan salmon* (*Oncorhynchus masou formosanum*) in central Taiwan's Chi Chia Wan Stream.
- Chinook salmon (*Oncorhynchus tshawytscha*) is also known in the USA as King or Blackmouth Salmon, and as Spring Salmon in British Columbia. Chinook are the largest of all Pacific salmon, frequently exceeding 30 lb (14 kg). The name Tyee is used in British Columbia to refer to Chinook over 30 pounds. Chinook salmon are known to range as far north as the Mackenzie River and Kugluktuk in the central Canadian arctic.
- Chum salmon (*Oncorhynchus keta*) is known as Dog, Keta, or Calico salmon in some parts of the USA. This species has the widest geographic range of the Pacific species: south to the Sacramento River in California in the eastern

Pacific and the island of Kyushu in the Sea of Japan in the western Pacific; north to the Mackenzie River in Canada in the east and to the Lena River in Siberia in the west.

Male Ocean Phase Coho Salmon

Coho salmon (*Oncorhynchus kisutch*) is also known in the USA as Silver salmon. This species is found throughout the coastal waters of Alaska and British Columbia and up most clear-running streams and rivers. It is also now known to occur, albeit infrequently, in the Mackenzie River.

Pink salmon (*Oncorhynchus gorbuscha*), known as humpies in south east and south west Alaska, are found from northern California and Korea, throughout the northern Pacific, and from the Mackenzie River in Canada to the Lena River in Siberia, usually in shorter coastal streams. It is the smallest of the Pacific species, with an average weight of 3.5 lb (1.6 kg) to 4 lb (1.8 kg).

Sockeye salmon (*Oncorhynchus nerka*) is also known in the USA as Red salmon. This lake-rearing species is found south as far as the Klamath River in California in the eastern Pacific and northern Hokkaido island in Japan in the western Pacific and as far north as Bathurst Inlet in the Canadian Arctic in the east and the Anadyr River in Siberia in the west. Although most adult Pacific salmon feed on small fish, shrimp and squid; sockeye feed on plankton that they filter through gill rakers Kokanee salmon is a land-locked form of sockeye salmon.

Other Species

The huchen or Danube salmon (*Hucho hucho*), the largest permanent fresh water salmonid species.

The salmon has long been at the heart of the culture and livelihood of coastal dwellers. Many people of the Northern Pacific shore had a ceremony to honor the first return of the year. For many centuries, people caught salmon as they swam upriver to spawn. A famous spearfishing site on the Columbia River at Celilo Falls was inundated after great dams were built on the river. The Ainu, of northern Japan, trained dogs to catch salmon as they returned to their breeding grounds *en masse*. Now, salmon are caught in bays and near shore.

Salmon population levels are of concern in the Atlantic and in some parts of the Pacific but in Alaska stocks are still abundant. Fish farming of Pacific salmon is outlawed in the United States Exclusive Economic Zone, however, there is a substantial network of publicly funded hatcheries, and the State of Alaska's fisheries management system is viewed as a leader in the management of wild fish stocks. Some of the most important Alaskan salmon sustainable wild fisheries are located near the Kenai River, Copper River, and in Bristol Bay. In Canada, returning Skeena River wild salmon support commercial, subsistence and recreational fisheries, as well as the area's diverse wildlife on the coast and around communities hundreds of miles inland in the watershed. The status of wild salmon in Washington is mixed. Out of 435 wild stocks of salmon and steelhead, only 187 of them were classified as healthy; 113 had an unknown status, 1 was extinct, 12 were in critical condition and 122 were experiencing depressed populations. The Columbia River salmon population is now less than 3 per cent of what it was when Lewis and Clark arrived at the river. The commercial salmon fisheries in California have been either severely curtailed or closed completely in recent years, due to critically low returns on the Klamath and or Sacramento Rivers, causing millions of dollars in losses to commercial fishermen. Both Atlantic and Pacific salmon are popular sportfish. Salmon populations now exist in all the Great Lakes. Coho stocks were planted in the late 1960s in response to the growing population of non-native alwifes by the state of Michigan. Now Chinook (King), Atlantic, and Coho (silver) salmon are annually stocked in all Great Lakes by mosts bordering states and provinces. These populations are not self sustaining and do not provide much in the way of a commercial fishery, but have led to the development of a thriving sportfishery.

Salmon aquaculture is the major economic contributor to the world production of farmed fin-fish, representing over

U$1 billion annually. Other commonly cultured fish species include: tilapia, catfish, sea bass, carp, bream, and trout. Salmon farming is very big in Chile, Norway, Scotland, Canada and the Faroe Islands, and is the source for most salmon consumed in America and Europe. Atlantic salmon are also, in very small volumes, farmed in Russia and the island of Tasmania, Australia.

Salmon are carnivorous and are currently fed a meal produced from catching other wild fish and other marine organisms. Salmon farming leads to a high demand for wild forage fish. Salmon require large nutritional intakes of protein, and consequently, farmed salmon consume more fish than they generate as a final product. To produce one pound of farmed salmon, products from several pounds of wild fish are fed to them. As the salmon farming industry expands, it requires more wild forage fish for feed, at a time when seventy five percent of the worlds monitored fisheries are already near to or have exceeded their maximum sustainable yield. The industrial scale extraction of wild forage fish for salmon farming then impacts the survivability of the wild predator fish who rely on them for food.

Work continues on substituting vegetable proteins for animal proteins in the salmon diet. Unfortunately though, this substitution results in lower levels of the highly valued Omega-3 content in the farmed product.

Intensive salmon farming now uses open-net cages which have low production costs but have the drawback of allowing disease and sea lice to spread to local wild salmon stocks.

On a dry-dry basis, it takes 2-4 kg of wild caught fish to produce one kg of salmon.

Another form of salmon production, which is safer but less controllable, is to raise salmon in hatcheries until they are old enough to become independent. They are then released into rivers, often in an attempt to increase the salmon population. This system is referred to as ranching and was very common in countries like Sweden before the Norwegians developed salmon farming, but is seldom done by private companies, as anyone may catch the salmon when they return to spawn, limiting a company's chances of benefiting financially from their investment. Because of this, the method has mainly been used by various public authorities and non profit groups like the Cook Inlet Aquaculture Association as a way of artificially increasing salmon populations in situations where they have declined due to overharvest, construction of dams, and habitat destruction or fragmentation. Unfortunately, there can be negative consequences to this sort of population manipulation, including genetic "dilution" of the wild stocks, and many jurisdictions are now beginning to discourage supplemental fish planting in favour of harvest controls and habitat improvement and protection. A variant method of fish stocking, called ocean ranching, is under development in Alaska. There, the young salmon are released into the ocean far from any wild salmon streams. When it is time for them to spawn, they return to where they were released where fishermen can then catch them.

An alternative method to hatcheries is to use spawning channels. These are artificial streams, usually parallel to an existing stream with concrete or rip-rap sides and gravel bottoms. Water from the adjacent stream is piped into the top of the channel, sometimes via a header pond to settle out sediment. Spawning success is often much better in channels than in adjacent streams due to the control of floods which in some years can wash out the natural redds. Because of the lack of floods, spawning channels must sometimes be cleaned out to remove accumulated sediment. The same floods which destroy natural redds also clean them out. Spawning channels preserve the natural selection of natural streams as there is no temptation, as in hatcheries, to use prophylactic chemicals to control diseases.

Farm raised salmon are fed the carotenoids astaxanthin and canthaxanthin, so that their flesh color matches wild salmon.

According to Canadian biologist Dorothy Kieser, myxozoan parasite *Henneguya salminicola* is commonly found in the flesh of salmonids. It has been recorded in the field samples of salmon returning to the Queen Charlotte Islands. The fish responds by walling off the parasitic infection into a number of cysts that contain milky fluid. This fluid is an accumulation of a large number of parasites.

Henneguya and other parasites in the myxosporean group have a complex lifecycle where the salmon is one of two hosts. The fish releases the spores after spawning. In the *Henneguya* case, the spores enter a second host, most likely an invertebrate, in the spawning stream. When juvenile salmon out-migrate to the Pacific Ocean, the second host releases a stage infective to salmon. The parasite is then carried in the salmon until the next spawning cycle. The myxosporean parasite that causes whirling disease in trout, has a similar lifecycle. However, as opposed to whirling disease, the *Henneguya* infestation does not appear to cause disease in the host salmon — even heavily infected fish tend to return to spawn successfully.

According to Dr. Kieser, a lot of work on *Henneguya salminicola* was done by scientists at the Pacific Biological Station in Nanaimo in the mid-1980s, in particular, an overview report which states that "the fish that have the longest fresh water residence time as juveniles have the most noticeable infections. Hence in order of prevalence coho are most infected followed by sockeye, chinook, chum and pink." As well, the report says that, at the time the studies were conducted, stocks from the middle and upper reaches of large river systems in British Columbia such as Fraser, Skeena, Nass and from mainland coastal streams in the southern half of B.C. "are more likely to have a low prevalence of infection." The report also states "It should be stressed that *Henneguya*, economically deleterious though it is, is harmless from the view of public health. It is strictly a fish parasite that cannot live in or affect warm blooded animals, including man".

According to Klaus Schallie, Molluscan Shellfish Program Specialist with the Canadian Food Inspection Agency, "*Henneguya salminicola* is found in southern B.C. also and in all species of salmon. I have previously examined smoked chum salmon sides that were riddled with cysts and some sockeye runs in Barkley Sound (southern B.C., west coast of Vancouver Island) are noted for their high incidence of infestation."

Sea lice, particularly *Lepeophtheirus salmonis* and various *Caligus* species, including *Caligus clemensi* and *Caligus rogercresseyi*, can cause deadly infestations of both farm-grown and wild salmon. Sea lice are ectoparasites which feed on mucus, blood, and skin, and migrate and latch onto the skin of wild salmon during free-swimming, planktonic *nauplii* and *copepodid* larval stages, which can persist for several days. Large numbers of highly populated, open-net salmon farms can create exceptionally large concentrations of sea lice; when exposed in river estuaries containing large numbers of open-net farms, many young wild salmon are infected, and do not survive as a result. Adult salmon may survive otherwise critical numbers of sea lice, but small, thin-skinned juvenile salmon migrating to sea are highly vulnerable. On the Pacific coast of Canada, the louse-induced mortality of pink salmon in some regions is commonly over 80 per cent.

The population of wild salmon declined markedly in recent decades, especially north Atlantic populations which spawn in the waters of western Europe and eastern Canada, and wild salmon in the Snake and Columbia River system in northwestern United States. The decline is attributed to the following factors:

- Disease transfer from open net cage salmon farming, especially sea lice. The European Commission (2002) concluded "The reduction of wild salmonid abundance is also linked to other factors but there is more and more scientific evidence establishing a direct link between the number of lice-infested wild fish and the presence of cages in the same estuary." It is reported that wild salmon on the west coast of Canada are being driven to extinction by sea lice from nearby salmon farms.

- For Atlantic salmon smolts, it takes as few as eight sea lice to kill the fish. On the Pacific Coast where the smolt are much smaller, only one or two can be critical, often resulting in death. In the Atlantic, sea lice have been a proven factor in both Norwegian and Scottish salmon declines. In the Western Atlantic there has been little research at sea, but sea lice numbers in the period post-2000 do not appear to be a significant factor in the critical decline of endangered inner Bay of Fundy salmon. The situation may have been different in the 1980s and 1990s, but we are unlikely ever to know the factual history in that regard.
- Overfishing in general but especially commercial netting in the Faroes and Greenland. Several seafood sustainability guides have recommendations on which salmon fisheries are sustainable and which have negative impacts on Salmon populations.
- Ocean and river warming which can delay spawning and accelerate transition to smolting.
- Ulcerative dermal necrosis (UDN) infections of the 1970s and 1980s which severely affected adult salmon in freshwater rivers.
- Loss of suitable freshwater habitat, especially degradation of stream pools and reduction of suitable material for the excavation of redds. Historically stream pools were, to a large extent, created by beavers. With the extirpation of the beaver, the nurturing function of these ponds was lost.
- Reduction of the retention of the nutrients brought by the returning adult salmon in stream pools. Without stream pools, dead adult salmon tend to be washed straight back down the streams and rivers.

- The construction of dams, weirs, barriers and other "flood prevention" measures, which bring severe adverse impacts to river habitat and on the accessibility of those habitats to salmon. This is particularly true in the northwest USA, where large numbers of dams have been built in many river systems, including over 400 in the Columbia River Basin.
- Other environmental factors such as light intensity, water flow, or change in temperature dramatically affects salmon during their migration season
- Loss of invertebrate diversity and population density in rivers because of modern farming methods and various sources of pollution, thus reducing food availability.
- Reduction in freshwater base flow in rivers and disruption of seasonal flows, because of diversions and extractions, hydroelectric power generation, irrigation schemes, barge transportation, and slackwater reservoirs, which inhibit normal migratory processes and increase predation for salmon.
- Loss of suitable low gradient stream habitats due to agricultural practices such as the removal of riparian plants, destabilization of stream banks by livestock and irrigation processes.

There are efforts to relieve this situation. As such, several governments and NGOs are sharing in research and habitat restoration efforts.

In the western Atlantic, the Atlantic Salmon Federation has developed a major sonic tracking technology programme to understand the high at-sea mortality since the early 1990s. Ocean arrays are deployed across the Baie des Chaleurs and between Newfoundland and Labrador at the Strait of Belle Isle. Salmon have now been tracked half way from rivers such as the Restigouche to Greenland feeding grounds. Now the first line of the Ocean Tracking Network initiative is installed by DFO and Dalhousie University of Halifax from Halifax to the edge of the continental shelf. First results include Atlantic salmon travelling from the Penobscot River in Maine, the "anchor river" for US Atlantic salmon populations.

In the northern Atlantic, the North Atlantic Salmon Fund, lead by Icelandic Entrepreneur Orri Vigfússon, has since 1989 worked closely with governments and fishermen for conservation. The conservation efforts are not limited to oceans, and a sustainable angling scheme has been developed in rivers, notably in Vopnafjörður, Iceland.

Results overall are showing that estuary problems exist for some rivers, but issues involving feeding grounds at sea are impacting populations as well. In 2008 returns were markedly improved for Atlantic salmon on both sides of the Atlantic Ocean, but no one knows if this is a temporary improvement or sign of a trend.

NOAA's Office of Protected Resources maintains a list of Endangered Species, the Endangered Species Act.

Sweden has generated a protection program as part of its Biodiversity Action Plan.

State of Salmon maintains an IUCN redlist of endangered salmon.

The Kamchatka Peninsula, in the Russian Far East, contains the world's greatest salmon sanctuary.

Bear Lake, Alaska, is the site of salmon enhancement activities since 1962.

Fishery Pressures

A great threat to Pacific salmon conservation is commercial fishing. There are many methods of harvest for the commercial salmon fishing industry, such as trolling, seining, and gillnetting. Gillnets are an extremely size-selective method of harvest, where a long net is placed in the path of the salmon's migration to their natal stream in hopes of entangling the salmon for commercial harvest. Gillnets are extremely size-selective; fish too small to be caught pass through the net, fish too large cannot be entangled, only catching fish that fall somewhere in between. By selectively harvesting certain sized fish, governed by the mesh-size of the gillnet, some age-class and length-class fish are selectively removed from the population, progressively leaving phenotypically smaller spawners. Fecundity generally decreases with length. So, smaller fish produce fewer eggs than larger fish. There is also concern regarding the genetic information passed down from the fish. If the majority of spawning fish in a particular salmon run has gotten smaller due to the size-selective fishing methods, the run could eventually evolve to become smaller.

Gillnet Size-Selectivity

Gillnets are designed to harvest a specific sized fish. For example, Washington Department of Fish and Wildlife's 2010 Commercial Regulations had a 7-inch minimum mesh size restriction for Chinook, and a 5-inch minimum – 5.5-inch maximum for sockeye. Gillnetting only targets the fish which are small enough to enter the net, but large enough to be tangled in it. Possible problems arising from this selective harvest are smaller reproducing adult fish, as well as the unexpected mortality of the fish which sustain injuries from the gillnet but are not retained in the fishery. Most salmon populations include several age classes, allowing for fish of different ages, and sizes, to reproduce with each other. A recent 2009 study looked at 59 years of catch and escapement data of Bristol Bay sockeye to determine age and size at maturity trends attributable to the selectivity of commercial gillnet harvests. The study found that the larger females (>550 mm) of all age classes were most susceptible to harvest. The study suggests that smaller, younger fish were more likely to successfully traverse the gillnet fishery and reproduce than the larger fish. The study also found that the average length of sockeye harvested from 1946 – 2005 was 8 mm larger than the sockeye who escaped the gillnet fishery to spawn, reducing the fecundity of the average female by 5 per cent, or 104 eggs.

Gillnet-Related Mortality

If a salmon enters a gillnet, but manages to escape, it often sustains injuries. These injuries can lead to a lower degree of reproductive success. A study aimed at quantifying mortality of Bristol Bay sockeye salmon due to gillnet-related injuries found that 11-29 per cent of sockeye sustained fishery-related injuries attributable to gillnets, 51 per cent of those fish were expected to not reproduce.

Salmon and Beavers

Beavers are archetypal ecosystem engineers; in the process of clear cutting and damming, beavers alter their ecosystem extensively. Beaver ponds can provide critical habitat for juvenile salmon. An example of this was seen in the years following 1818 in the Columbia River Basin. In 1818, the British government made an agreement with the U.S. government to allow U.S. citizens access to the Columbia catchment. At the time, the Hudson's Bay Company sent word to trappers to extirpate all furbearers from the area in an effort to make the area less attractive to U.S. fur traders. In response to the elimination of beavers from large parts of the river system, salmon runs plummeted, even in the absence of many of the factors usually associated with the demise of salmon runs. Salmon recruitment can be affected by beavers' dams because dams can:

- Slow the rate at which nutrients are flushed from the system; nutrients provided by adult salmon dying throughout the fall and winter remain available in the spring to newly-hatched juveniles.
- Provide deeper water pools where young salmon can avoid avian predators.
- Increase productivity through photosynthesis and by enhancing the conversion efficiency of the cellulose-powered detritus cycle.
- Create low-energy environments where juvenile salmon put the food they ingest into growth rather than into fighting currents.

- Increase structural complexity with many physical niches where salmon can avoid predators

Beavers' dams are able to nurture salmon juveniles in Estuarine tidal marshes where the salinity is less than 10ppm. Beavers build small dams of generally less than 2 feet (0.61 m) high in channels in the Myrtle zone. These dams can be overtopped at high tide and hold water at low tide. This provides refuges for juvenile salmon so they don't have to swim into large channels where they are subject to predation.

Salmon as Food

Salmon is a popular food. Classified as an "oily fish", salmon is considered to be healthy due to the fish's high protein, high omega-3 fatty acids, and high vitamin D content. Salmon is also a source of cholesterol, with a range of 23-214 mg/100 g depending on the species. According to reports in the journal *Science*, however, farmed salmon may contain high levels of dioxins. PCB (polychlorinated biphenyl) levels may be up to eight times higher in farmed salmon than in wild salmon. Omega-3 content may also be lower than in wild-caught specimens, and in a different proportion to what is found naturally. Omega-3 comes in three types, ALA, DHA and EPA; wild salmon has traditionally been an important source of DHA and EPA, which are important for brain function and structure, among other things. This means if the farmed salmon is fed on a meal which is partially grain, then the amount of omega-3 it contains will be present as ALA (alpha-linolenic acid). The body can itself convert ALA omega-3 into DHA and EPA, but at a very inefficient rate (2-15%). Nonetheless, according to a 2006 study published in the Journal of the American Medical Association, the benefits of eating even farmed salmon still outweigh any risks imposed by contaminants. The type of omega-3 present may not be a factor for other important health functions.

A simple rule of thumb is that the vast majority of Atlantic salmon available on the world market are farmed (greater than 99%), whereas the majority of Pacific salmon are wild caught (greater than 80%). Farmed Atlantic salmon outnumber wild Atlantic salmon 85-to-1.

Salmon flesh is generally orange to red, although there are some examples of white-fleshed wild salmon. The natural colour of salmon results from carotenoid pigments, largely astaxanthin but also canthaxanthin, in the flesh. Wild salmon get these carotenoids from eating krill and other tiny shellfish. Because consumers have shown a reluctance to purchase white-fleshed salmon, astaxanthin (E161j), and very minutely canthaxanthin (E161g), are added as artificial colorants to the feed of farmed salmon, because prepared diets do not naturally contain these pigments. In most cases, the astaxanthin is made chemically; alternatively it is extracted from shrimp flour. Another possibility is the use of dried red yeast, which provides the same pigment. However, synthetic mixtures are the least expensive option. Astaxanthin is a potent antioxidant that stimulates the development of healthy fish nervous systems and enhances the fish's fertility and growth rate. Research has revealed canthaxanthin may have negative effects on the human eye, accumulating in the retina at high levels of consumption. Today, the concentration of carotenoids (mainly canthaxanthin and astaxanthin) exceeds 8 mg/kg of flesh, and all fish producers try to reach a level that represents a value of 16 on the "Roche Color Card", a colour card used to show how pink the fish will appear at specific doses. This scale is specific for measuring the pink colour due to astaxanthin and is not for the orange hue obtained with canthaxanthin. The development of processing and storage operations, which can be detrimental on canthaxanthin flesh concentration, has led to an increased quantity of pigments added to the diet to compensate for the degrading effects of the processing. In wild fish, carotenoid levels of up to 25 mg are present, but levels of canthaxanthin are, in contrast, minor. Canned salmon in the U.S. is usually wild Pacific catch, though some farmed salmon is available in canned form. Smoked salmon is another popular preparation method, and can either be hot or cold smoked. Lox can refer either to cold smoked salmon or to salmon cured in a brine solution (also called gravlax). Traditional canned salmon includes some skin (which is harmless) and bone (which adds calcium). Skinless and boneless canned salmon is also available.

Raw salmon flesh may contain *Anisakis* nematodes, marine parasites that cause Anisakiasis. Before the availability of refrigeration, the Japanese did not consume raw salmon. Salmon and salmon roe have only recently come into use in making sashimi (raw fish) and sushi.

The salmon is an important creature in several strands of Celtic mythology and poetry, which often associated them with wisdom and venerability. In Irish mythology, a creature called the Salmon of Wisdom (or the Salmon of Knowledge) plays key role in the tale known as *The Boyhood Deeds of Fionn*. The Salmon will grant powers of knowledge to whoever eats it, and has been sought by the poet Finn Eces for seven years. Finally Finn Eces catches the fish and gives it to his young pupil, Fionn mac Cumhaill, to prepare it for him. However, Fionn burns his thumb on the salmon's juices, and he instinctively puts it in his mouth. As such, he inadvertently gains the Salmon's wisdom. Elsewhere in Irish mythology, the salmon is also one of the incarnations of both Tuan mac Cairill and Fintan mac Bóchra.

Salmon also feature in Welsh mythology. In the prose tale *Culhwch and Olwen*, the Salmon of Llyn Llyw is the oldest animal in Britain, and the only creature who knows the location of Mabon ap Modron. After speaking to a string of other ancient animals who do not know his whereabouts, King Arthur's men Cai and Bedwyr are led to the Salmon of Llyn Llyw, who lets them ride its back to the walls of Mabon's prison in Gloucester.

In Norse mythology, after Loki tricked the blind god Höðr into killing his brother Baldr, Loki jumped into a river and transformed himself into a salmon in order to escape punishment from the other gods. When they held out a net to trap him he attempted to leap over it but was caught by Thor who grabbed him by the tail with his hand, and this is why the salmon's tail is tapered.

Salmon are central to Native American mythology on the Pacific coast, from the Haida to the Nootka.

CHAPTER 12

Aquaculture of Salmon

Salmon, along with carp, are the two most important fish groups in aquaculture. In 2007, the aquaculture of salmon and salmon trout was worth US$10.7 billion. The most commonly farmed salmon is the Atlantic salmon. Other commonly farmed fish groups include tilapia, catfish, sea bass, bream and trout.

Salmon aquaculture production grew over ten-fold during the 25 years from 1982 to 2007. Leading producers of farmed salmon are Norway with 33 per cent, Chile with 31 per cent, and other European producers with 19 per cent.

There is currently much controversy about the ecological and health impacts of intensive salmon aquaculture. There are particular concerns about the impacts on wild salmon and other marine life. Much of this controversy is part of a major commercial competitive fight for market share and price between Alaska commercial salmon fishermen and the rapidly evolving salmon aquaculture industry.

The aquaculture of salmon is the farming and harvesting of salmon under controlled conditions. Farmed salmon can be contrasted with wild salmon captured using commercial fishing techniques. However, the concept of "wild" salmon as used by the Alaska Seafood Marketing Institute includes stock enhancement fish produced in hatcheries that have historically been considered ocean ranching. The percentage of the Alaska salmon harvest resulting from ocean ranching depends upon the species of salmon and location, however it is all marketed as "wild Alaska salmon".

Methods of salmon aquaculture originated in late 18th century fertilization trials in Europe. In the late 19th century, salmon hatcheries were used in Europe and North America. From the late 1950s, enhancement programmes based on hatcheries were established in the United States, Canada, Japan and the USSR. The contemporary technique using floating sea cages originated in Norway in the late 1960s.

Salmon are usually farmed in two stages and in some places maybe more. First, the salmon are hatched from eggs and raised on land in freshwater tanks. When they are 12 to 18 months old, the smolt (juvenile salmon) are transferred to floating sea cages or net pens anchored in sheltered bays or fjords along a coast. This farming in a marine environment is known as mariculture. There they are fed pelleted feed for another 12 to 24 months, when they are harvested.

Norway produces 33 per cent of the world's farmed salmon, and Chile produces 31 per cent. The coastlines of these countries have suitable water temperatures and many areas well protected from storms. Chile is close to large forage fisheries which supply fish meal for salmon aquaculture. Scotland and Canada are also significant producers.

Modern salmon farming systems are intensive and not usually owned by small scale operators. Their ownership is often under the control of agribusiness corporations, operating mechanised assembly lines on an industrial scale producing standardised products. In 2003, nearly half of the world's farmed salmon was produced by just five companies.

Modern commercial hatcheries for supplying salmon smolts to aquaculture net pens have been shifting to Recycle

Aquaculture Systems (RAS) where the water is recycled within the hatchery. This allows location of the hatchery to be independent of a significant fresh water supply and allows economical temperature control to both speed up and slow down the growth rate to match the needs of the net pens.

Conventional hatchery systems operate flow through where spring water or other water source flow into the hatchery. The eggs are then hatched in trays and the salmon smolts produced in raceways. The waste products from the growing salmon fry and the feed are usually discharged into the local river. Conventional flow through hatcheries, such as are being used by most of the Alaska ocean ranching enhancement hatcheries use more than 100 tons of water to produce to produce a kg of smolts. An alternative method to hatching in freshwater tanks is to use spawning channels.

These are artificial streams, usually parallel to an existing stream with concrete or rip-rap sides and gravel bottoms. Water from the adjacent stream is piped into the top of the channel, sometimes via a header pond to settle out sediment. Spawning success is often much better in channels than in adjacent streams due to the control of floods which in some years can wash out the natural redds. Because of the lack of floods, spawning channels must sometimes be cleaned out to remove accumulated sediment.

The same floods which destroy natural redds also clean them out. Spawning channels preserve the natural selection of natural streams as there is no temptation, as in hatcheries, to use prophylactic chemicals to control diseases. However, exposing fish to wild parasites and pathogens using uncontrolled water supplies, combined with the high cost of spawning channels, makes this technology unsuitable for salmon aquaculture businesses. This type of technology is only useful for stock enhancement programmes.

Sea Cages

Sea cages, or net pens, are usually made of mesh framed with steel or plastic. They can be square or circular, 10 to 32 metres across and 10 metres deep, with volumes between 1,000 and 10,000 cubic metres. A large sea cage can house up to 90,000 fish.

They are usually placed side by side to form a system called a *seafarm* or *seasite*, with a floating wharf and walkways along the net boundaries. Additional nets can also surround the seafarm to keep out predatory marine mammals. Stocking densities range from 8 to 18 kilograms per cubic metre for Atlantic salmon and 5 to 10 kilograms per cubic metre for Chinook salmon.

In contrast to closed or recirculating systems, the open net cages of salmon farming lower production costs, but provide no effective barrier to the discharge of wastes, parasites and disease into the surrounding coastal waters. Farmed salmon in open net cages can escape into wild habitats, for example, during storms.

An emerging wave in aquaculture is applying the same farming methods used for salmon to other carnivorous finfish species, such as cod, bluefin tuna, halibut and snapper. However, this is likely to have the same environmental drawbacks as salmon farming.

Feeding

Salmon are carnivorous and are currently being fed compound fish feeds containing fish meal and other feed ingredients, ranging from wheat byproducts to soybean meal and feather meal. Being an aquatic carnivore, salmon don't tolerate or properly metabolize many plant based carbohydrates and use fats instead of carbohydrates as a primary energy source. With the amount of world wide fish meal production being almost a constant amount for the last 30+ years and at maximum sustainable yield (MSY), much of the fish meal market has shifted from chicken and pig feed to fish and shrimp feeds as aquaculture has grown in this time period.

Work continues on substituting vegetable proteins and protein concentrates for fish meal in the salmon diet. Many substitutions for fish meal are known and diets containing zero fish meal are possible. However, commercial economic animal diets are determined by least cost linear programming models that are effectively competing with similar models for chicken and pig feeds for the same feed ingredients and these models show that fish meal is more useful in aquatic diets than in chicken diets, where they can make the chickens taste like fish . Unfortunately though, this substitution can result in lower levels of the highly valued omega-3 content in the farmed product. However, when vegetable oil is used in the growing diet as an energy source and a different finishing diet containing high omega-3 content fatty acids from either fish oil, algae oils or some vegetable oils are used a few months before harvest, this problem is eliminated.

At the present time, more than 50 per cent of the world fish oil production is feed to farmed salmon. Farm raised salmon are also fed the carotenoids astaxanthin and canthaxanthin, so that their flesh color matches wild salmon, which also contain the same carotenoid pigments from their diet in the wild. On a dry-dry basis, it takes 2-4 kg of wild caught fish to produce one kg of salmon. Wild salmon require about 10kg of forage fish to produce a kg of salmon, as part of the normal trophic level energy transfer. The difference between the two numbers is related to farmed salmon feed containing other ingredients beyond fish meal and the fact that farmed fish don't spend a lot of metabolic energy catching a dinner that doesn't want to be caught.

Harvesting

Modern harvesting methods are shifting towards using wet well ships to transport the live salmon to the processing plant. This allows the fish to be killed, bleed, and filleted before rigor has occurred. This results in superior product quality to the customer along with more humane processing.

To obtain maximum quality, it is necessary to minimize the level of stress in the live salmon until actually being electrically and percussively killed and the gills slit for bleeding. These improvements in processing time and freshness to the final customer are commercially significant and forcing the commercial wild fisheries to upgrade their processing to the benefit of all seafood consumers. An older method of harvesting is to use a sweep net, which operates a bit like a purse seine net. The sweep net is a big net with weights along the bottom edge. It is stretched across the pen with the bottom edge extending to the bottom of the pen. Lines attached to the bottom corners are raised, herding some fish into the purse, where they are netted. Before killing, the fish are usually rendered unconscious in water saturated in carbon dioxide, although this practice is being phased out in some countries due to ethical and product quality concerns. More advanced systems use a percussive-stun harvest system that kills the fish instantly and humanely with a blow to the head from a pneumatic piston. They are then bled by cutting the gill arches and immediately immersing them in iced water. Harvesting and killing methods are designed to minimise scale loss, and avoid the fish releasing stress hormones, which negatively affect flesh quality.

Wild salmon are captured from wild habitats using commercial fishing techniques. Most wild salmon is caught in North American, Japanese and Russian fisheries. The following table shows the changes in production of wild salmon and farmed salmon over a period of 25 years, as reported by the FAO. Russia, Japan and Alaska all operate major hatchery based stock enhancement programs that are really ocean ranching. The resulting fish hatchery fish are defined as "wild" for FAO and marketing purposes.

There is currently much controversy about the ecological and health impacts of intensive salmon aquaculture. There are particular concerns about the impacts on wild salmon and other marine life and on the incomes of commercial salmon fishermen. The interest of the commercial fishermen are trying to prevent competition.

Disease and Parasites

In 1972, Gyrodactylus, a monogenean parasite, spread from Norwegian hatcheries to wild salmon, and devastated some wild salmon populations.

In 1984, infectious salmon anemia (ISAv) was discovered in Norway in an Atlantic salmon hatchery. Eighty per cent of the fish in the outbreak died. ISAv, a viral disease, is now a major threat to the viability of Atlantic salmon farming. It is now the first of the diseases classified on List One of the European Commission's fish health regime. Amongst other measures, this requires the total eradication of the entire fish stock should an outbreak of the disease be confirmed on any farm. ISAv seriously affects salmon farms in Chile, Norway, Scotland and Canada, causing major economic losses to infected farms. As the name implies, it causes severe anemia of infected fish. Unlike mammals, the red blood cells of fish have DNA, and can become infected with viruses. The fish develop pale gills, and may swim close to the water surface, gulping for air. However, the disease can also develop without the fish showing any external signs of illness, the fish maintain a normal appetite, and then they suddenly die.

The disease can progress slowly throughout an infected farm and, in the worst cases, death rates may approach 100 per cent. It is also a threat to the dwindling stocks of wild salmon. Management strategies include developing a vaccine and improving genetic resistance to the disease.

In the wild, diseases and parasites are normally at low levels, and kept in check by natural predation on weakened individuals. In crowded net pens they can become epidemics. Diseases and parasites also transfer from farmed to wild salmon populations. A recent study in British Columbia links the spread of parasitic sea lice from river salmon farms to wild pink salmon in the same river.

The European Commission concluded "The reduction of wild salmonid abundance is also linked to other factors but there is more and more scientific evidence establishing a direct link between the number of lice-infested wild fish and the presence of cages in the same estuary." It is reported that wild salmon on the west coast of Canada are being driven to extinction by sea lice from nearby salmon farms. These predictions have been disputed by other scientists and recent harvests have indicated that the predictions were in error. Antibiotics and pesticides are often used to control the diseases and parasites.

Salmon farms are typically sited in marine ecosystems with good water quality, high water exchange rates, current speeds fast enough to prevent pollution of the bottom but slow enough to prevent pen damage, protection from major storms, reasonable water depth and a reasonable distance from major infrastructure such as ports, processing plants and logistical facilities like airports. Logistical considerations are significant and feed and maintenance labor must be transported to the facility and the product returned. Siting decisions are complicated by complex politically driven permitting problems in many countries that prevents optimal locations for the farms.

In sites without adequate currents there can be an accumulation of heavy metals on the benthos (seafloor) near the salmon farms, particularly copper and zinc.

Toxins are also found in the flesh of farmed salmon. A 2004 study, reported in *Science*, analysed farmed and wild salmon for organochlorine contaminants. They found the contaminants were higher in farmed salmon. Within the farmed salmon, European (particularly Scottish) salmon had the highest levels, and Chilean salmon the lowest.

A follow up study confirmed this, and found levels of dioxins, chlorinated pesticides, PCBs and other toxins up to ten times greater in farmed salmon than wild Pacific salmon. On a positive note, further research using the same fish samples used in the previous study, showed that farmed salmon contained levels of beneficial fatty acids that were two to three times higher than wild salmon. A follow up benefit-risk analysis on salmon consumption balanced the cancer risks with the (n-3) fatty acid advantages of salmon consumption. They found that recommended levels of (n-3) fatty acid consumption can be achieved eating farmed salmon with acceptable carcinogenic risks, but recommended levels of EPA+DHA intake cannot be achieved solely from farmed (or wild) salmon without unacceptable carcinogenic risks. The conclusions were that:

> "...consumers should not eat farmed fish from Scotland, Norway and eastern Canada more than three times a year; farmed fish from Maine, western Canada and Washington state no more than three to six times a year; and farmed fish from Chile no more than about six times a year. Wild chum salmon can be consumed safely as often as once a week, pink salmon, Sockeye and Coho about twice a month and Chinook just under once a month."

Farmed salmon can, and often do, escape from sea cages. If the farmed salmon is not native, it can compete with native wild species for food and habitat. If the farmed salmon is native, it can interbreed with the wild native salmon. Such interbreeding can reduce genetic diversity, disease resistance and adaptability. In 2004, about 500,000 salmon and trout escaped from ocean net pens off Norway. Around Scotland, 600,000 salmon were released during storms. Commercial fishermen targeting wild salmon not infrequently catch escaped farm salmon. At one stage, in the Faroe Islands, 20 to 40 per cent of all fish caught were escaped farm salmon.

Sea lice, particularly *Lepeophtheirus salmonis* and various *Caligus* species, including *Caligus clemensi* and *Caligus rogercresseyi*, can cause deadly infestations of both farm-grown and wild salmon. Sea lice are ectoparasites which feed on mucous, blood, and skin, and migrate and latch onto the skin of wild salmon during free-swimming, planktonic *nauplii* and *copepodid* larval stages, which can persist for several days.

Large numbers of highly populated, open-net salmon farms can create exceptionally large concentrations of sea lice;

when exposed in river estuaries containing large numbers of open-net farms, many young wild salmon are infected, and do not survive as a result. Adult salmon may survive otherwise critical numbers of sea lice, but small, thin-skinned juvenile salmon migrating to sea are highly vulnerable. On the Pacific coast of Canada, the louse-induced mortality of pink salmon in some regions is commonly over 80 per cent.

A 2008 meta-analysis of available data shows that salmon farming reduces the survival of associated wild salmon populations. This relationship has been shown to hold for Atlantic, steelhead, pink, chum, and coho salmon. The decrease in survival or abundance often exceeds 50 per cent. However, these studies are all correlation analysis and correlation doesn't equal causation, especially when similar salmon declines were occurring in Oregon and California, which have no salmon aquaculture or marine net pens. Independent of the predictions of the failure of salmon runs in Canada indicated by these studies, the wild salmon run in 2010 was a record harvest.

Wild salmon are anadromous. They spawn inland in fresh water and when young migrate to the ocean where they grow up. Most salmon return to the river where they were born, although some stray to other rivers. There is concern about of the role of genetic diversity within salmon runs. The resilience of the population depends on some fish being able to survive environmental shocks, such as unusual temperature extremes. It is also unclear what the effect of hatchery production has been on the genetic diversity of salmon.

Salmon have been genetically modified in laboratories so they can grow faster. There is opposition to the commercial use of these fish, and, so far, no approval has been given. A Canadian company, Aqua Bounty Farms, has developed a modified Atlantic salmon which grows several times faster, and is more disease resistant and cold tolerant.

This was achieved using a chinook salmon gene sequence affecting growth hormones, and a promoter sequence from the ocean pout affecting antifreeze production. Normally, salmon produce growth hormones only in the presence of light. The modified salmon doesn't switch growth hormone production off. The company first submitted the salmon for FDA approval in 1996. A concern with transgenic salmon is what might happen if they escape into the wild. One study, in a laboratory setting, found that modified salmon mixed with their wild cohorts were aggressive in competing, but ultimately failed.

Impact on Forage Fish

The use of forage fish for fish meal production has been almost a constant for the last thirty years and at the maximum sustainable yield, while the market for fish meal has shifted from chicken, pig and pet food to aquaculture diets. The fact that this market shift at constant production is an economic decision having no impact on the forage fish harvest rates for fish meal implies that the development of salmon aquaculture had no impact on forage fish harvest rates.

Fish do not actually produce omega-3 fatty acids, but instead accumulate them from either consuming microalgae that produce these fatty acids, as is the case with forage fish like herring and sardines, or, as is the case with fatty predatory fish, like salmon, by eating prey fish that have accumulated omega-3 fatty acids from microalgae. To satisfy this requirement, more than 50 per cent of the world fish oil production is fed to farmed salmon.

In addition, salmon require nutritional intakes of protein, protein which is often supplied to them in the form of fish meal as the lowest cost alternative protein. Consequently, farmed salmon consume more fish than they generate as a final product. To produce one pound of farmed salmon, products from several pounds of wild fish are fed to them. As the salmon farming industry expands, it requires a higher percentage of the wild forage fish for feed, at a time when seventy five per cent of the worlds monitored fisheries are already near to or have exceeded their maximum sustainable yield.

In 2004 the World Wide Fund for Nature (WWF) initiated the *Salmon Aquaculture Dialogue*. The aim of the dialogue is to produce an environmental standard for farmed salmon by 2010. The WWF have identified what they call "seven key environmental and social impacts", which they characterise as follows:

1. **Benthic impacts and siting**: Chemicals and excess nutrients from food and feces associated with salmon farms can disturb the flora and fauna on the ocean bottom (benthos).
2. **Chemical inputs**: Excessive use of chemicals - such as antibiotics, anti-foulants and pesticides - or the use of banned chemicals can have unintended consequences for marine organisms and human health.
3. **Disease/parasites**: Viruses and parasites can transfer between farmed and wild fish, as well as among farms.
4. **Escapes**: Escaped farmed salmon can compete with wild fish and interbreed with local wild stocks of the same population, altering the overall pool of genetic diversity.
5. **Feed**: A growing salmon farming business must control and reduce its dependency upon fishmeal and fishoil - a primary ingredient in salmon feed - so as not to put additional pressure on the world's fisheries. Fish caught to make fishmeal and oil currently represent one-third of the global fish harvest.
6. **Nutrient loading and carrying capacity**: Excess food and fish waste in the water have the potential to increase the levels of nutrients in the water. This can cause the growth of algae, which consumes oxygen that is meant for other plant and animal life.
7. **Social issues**: Salmon farming often employs a large number of workers on farms and in processing plants, potentially placing labor practices and worker rights under public scrutiny. Additionally, conflicts can arise among users of the shared coastal environment.

Another form of salmon production, which is safer but less controllable, is to raise salmon in hatcheries until they are old enough to become independent. They are then released into rivers, often in an attempt to increase the salmon population. This practice was very common in countries like Sweden before the Norwegians developed salmon farming, but is seldom done by private companies, as anyone may catch the salmon when they return to spawn, limiting a company's chances of benefiting financially from their investment.

Because of this, the method has mainly been used by various public authorities and non profit groups like the Cook Inlet Aquaculture Association as a way of artificially increasing salmon populations in situations where they have declined due to overharvest, construction of dams, and habitat destruction or disruption. Unfortunately, there can be negative consequences to this sort of population manipulation, including genetic "dilution" of the wild stocks, and many jurisdictions are now beginning to discourage supplemental fish planting in favour of harvest controls and habitat improvement and protection. A variant method of fish stocking, called ocean ranching, is under development in Alaska. There, the young salmon are released into the ocean far from any wild salmon streams. When it is time for them to spawn, they return to where they were released where fishermen can then catch them.

Atlantic Salmon

In their natal streams, Atlantic salmon are considered a prized recreational fish, pursued by avid fly anglers during its annual runs. At one time, the species supported an important commercial fishery and a supplemental food fishery. However, the wild Atlantic salmon fishery is commercially dead; after extensive habitat damage and overfishing, wild fish make up only 0.5 per cent of the Atlantic salmon available in world fish markets. The rest are farmed, predominantly from aquaculture in Chile, Canada, Norway, Russia, the UK and Tasmania in Australia.

Atlantic salmon is, by far, the species most often chosen for farming. It is easy to handle, it grows well in sea cages, commands a high market value and it adapts well to being farmed away from its native habitats.

Adult male and female fish are anaesthetised. Eggs and sperm are "stripped", after the fish are cleaned and cloth dried. Sperm and eggs are mixed, washed, and placed into fresh water. Adults recover in flowing, clean, well aerated water. Some researchers have even studied cryopreservation of their eggs.

Fry are generally reared in large freshwater tanks for 12 to 20 months. Once the fish have reached the smolt phase, they are taken out to sea where they are held for up to two years. During this time the fish grow and mature in large cages off the coasts of Canada, the USA, or parts of Europe.

Generally, cages are made of two nets. Inner nets, which wrap around the cages, hold the salmon. Outer nets, which are held by floats, keep predators out.

Many Atlantic salmon escape from cages at sea. Those salmon who further breed tend to lessen the genetic diversity of the species leading to lower survival rates, and lower catch rates. On the West Coast of Northern America, the non-native salmon can be an invasive threat, especially in Alaska and parts of Canada. This causes them to compete with native salmon for resources. Extensive efforts are underway to prevent escapes and the spread of Atlantic salmon in the Pacific and elsewhere.

Atlantic salmon which have escaped from the aquaculture industry have also been found breeding in rivers tributary to the Pacific Ocean in British Columbia on Canada's west coast.

Worldwide, in 2007, 1,433,708 tonnes of Atlantic salmon were harvested with a value of 7.578 billion US dollars.

In 1992 the salmon trout, *Salmo gairdneri,* was reclassified as a true salmon, *Oncorhynchus mykiss*. Salmon trout take an anadromous form and a non-anadromous form. The anadromous form, who migrate between lakes and rivers and the ocean, are known as steelhead salmon or ocean trout, while the non-anadromous form, who spend their entire life in freshwater, are known as rainbow trout.

Salmon trout are raised in many countries throughout the world. Since the 1950s production has grown exponentially, particularly in Europe and recently in Chile. Worldwide, in 2007, 604,695 tonnes of farmed salmon trout were harvested with a value of 2.589 billion US dollars. The largest producer is Chile. In Chile and Norway, the ocean cage production of steelhead has expanded to supply export markets. Inland production of rainbow trout to supply domestic markets has increased strongly in countries such as Italy, France, Germany, Denmark and Spain. Other significant producing countries include the USA, Iran, Germany and the UK.

Salmon trout have tender flesh and a mild, somewhat nutty flavour. Steelhead meat is pink like that of other salmon, and is more flavourful than the light-coloured meat of rainbow trout. Both are highly desired food. However, farmed trout and those taken from certain lakes have a pronounced earthy flavour which many people find unappealing; many shoppers therefore make it a point to ascertain the source of the fish before buying. Salmon trout that are wild have a diet of scuds (freshwater shrimp), insects such as flies, and crayfish are the most appealing. Dark red/orange meat indicates that it is either an anadromous steelhead or a farmed rainbow trout given a supplemental diet with a high iodine content. The resulting pink flesh is marketed under monikers like Ruby Red or Carolina Red.

The salmon trout is especially susceptible to enteric redmouth disease. There has been considerable research conducted on redmouth disease, as its implications for salmon trout farmers are significant. The disease does not affect humans.

Coho Salmon

The Coho salmon is the state animal of Chiba, Japan.

Coho salmon mature after only one year in the sea, so two separate broodstocks (spawners) are needed, alternating each year. Broodfish are selected from the salmon in the seasites and transferred to freshwater tanks for maturation and spawning."

Worldwide, in 2007, 115,376 tonnes of farmed Coho salmon were harvested with a value of 456 million US dollars. Chile, with about 90 per cent of word production, is the primary producer with Japan and Canada producing the rest.

Chinook Salmon

In Alaska, Chinook salmon are the state fish, and are known as "king salmon" because of their large size and flavoursome flesh. Those from the Copper River in Alaska are particularly known for their colour, rich flavour, firm texture, and high Omega-3 oil content.

Worldwide, in 2007, 11,542 tonnes of farmed Chinook salmon were harvested with a value of 83 million US dollars. New Zealand is the largest producer of farmed king salmon, accounting for over half of world production (7,400 tonnes in 2005). Most of the salmon are farmed in the sea (mariculture) using a method sometimes called sea-cage ranching. Sea-cage ranching takes place in large floating net cages, about 25 metres across and 15 metres deep, moored to the sea floor in clean, fast-flowing coastal waters. Smolt (young fish) from freshwater hatcheries are transferred to cages containing several thousand salmon, and remain there for the rest of their life. They are fed fishmeal pellets high in protein and oil.

King salmon are also farmed in net cages placed in freshwater rivers or raceways, using techniques similar to those used for sea-farmed salmon. A unique form of freshwater salmon farming occurs in some hydroelectric canals. A site in Tekapo, fed by fast cold waters from the

Southern Alps, is the highest salmon farm in the world, 677 metres above sea level.

Before they are killed, cage salmon are anaesthetised with a herbal extract. They are then spiked in the brain. The heart beats for a time as the animal is bled from its sliced gills. Relaxing the salmon like this when it is killed produces firm, long-keeping flesh. Lack of disease in wild populations and low stocking densities used in the cages means that New Zealand salmon farmers do not use antibiotics and chemicals that are often needed elsewhere.

CHAPTER 13

Live Food Fish Trade

The live food fish trade is a global system that links fishing communities with markets, primarily in Hong Kong and mainland China. Many of the fish are captured on coral reefs in Southeast Asia or the Pacific Island nations.

Live fish trade has two parts to it, both food fish (for dinner) as well as ornamental fish (for aquariums). While the fish can come from many places, the majority comes from Southeast Asia.

Within the live food trade there are certain types of fish demanded more often by consumers, particularly smaller and medium-sized fish. According to the book While Stocks Last: The Live Reef Food Fish Trade consumer demand has caused the fish captured on coral reefs to be the most valued fish in the trade. Consumers are important because they are directly purchasing these fish species at restaurants and stores. In addition to these types of fishes, many juvenile fish are used for the live food trade. There are also cultural and regional preferences among consumers, for example, Chinese consumers often prefer their fish to be reddish in color believing the color to be auspicious (Sadovy, Y.J, 393). These preferences inevitably affect the biodiversity of marine life making certain fish species rarer to find.

The life fish food trade is a lucrative business. According to University of Washington Professor Patrick Christie, live fish caught for food export earns approximately $6000 a ton. To help support themselves and their families, fishermen in Oceania and Southeast Asia sometimes use illegal fishing methods. Although many feel the fish are worth the cost, a typical dinner can cost up to one hundred dollars per kilogram. The wholesale value on these fish is anywhere from eleven US dollars to sixty-three US dollars per kilogram, meaning there's a large markup and resale value. (Hong Kong alone is estimated to be about four hundred million US dollars a year.) A large part of the live food fish trade is that there is a lot of money being made here. Because this trade frequently uses illegal methods of collecting (using cyanide), there is no way to know for sure how much money is being made each year on live fish trade, although estimates conclude probably over one billion US dollars each year.

As is often the case, consumers are willing to pay large amounts of money on rare and fresh fish. One 500-pound, polka-dot grouper, estimated to be more than a century old, was hacked into fillets by seven kitchen workers in about half an hour, the Economist reports. It was expected to bring about $15,000.

The centre for the Live Food Fish Trade is located in Hong Kong — the markets consumers contribute $400 million to the estimated $1 billion of the trades global value (Seaweb). Total imports flowing into Hong Kong included 10153 metric tons, of which 30 per cent was re-exported to mainland China (Montaldi). Other major markets include Singapore, mainland China, and Taiwan (Graham). The primary suppliers of wild caught fish are Indonesia (accounting for nearly 50 per cent of Hong Kong's imports), Thailand, Malaysia, Australia, and Vietnam (Graham). However, Taiwan and Malaysia are leading the charge towards farmed live fish specializing in an industry that "harvested annually has probably been in the billions [Metric Tons](Graham)." Farming live fish is gaining popularity as tastes for live fish are burgeoning across South Asia and countries look to become more and more self sustainable, this is appareant in nations with sizable Chinese populations such as Indonesia and Malaysia.

Hong Kong and China are the dominant markets for the live fish, in addition to other cities in the region that have large Chinese populations, including Singapore and Kuala Lumpur. In Southeast Asia, Singapore alone consumes 500 tons of live coral fish a year. Exports from Southeast Asia rose to over 5,000 tons in 1995 from 400 tons in 1989. However, in 1996, exports declined by 22 per cent. Indonesia, which accounts for over 60 per cent of the harvest, saw exports falling by over 450 tons. That same year, other Southeast Asian countries have experienced similar drops in stocks of live coral fish for food. In 1996, the Philippines' exports were halved, while Malaysian exports declined by over 30 per cent. These decreases in catch have been due to the excessive amount of fish caught for exports and the degradation of the coral reefs from such procedures.

Corruption in the Trade

The live fish trade is a complex issue that involves many different perspectives, all of which must be considered in trying to approach a solution. While, at first, one may point the finger at the fishermen themselves as the criminals, there are many other factors. One is the economic disparity of many of the communities that take part in cyanide, dynamite, or other illegal fishing practices. 40 per cent of the Filipino population and 27 per cent of the Indonesian population is considered to be in poverty. Many whose livelihood once depended on fishing or agriculture are realizing it is more lucrative to participate in illegal fishing activities.

Community members who are not a part of the trade are affected by the activities of these illegal fishers. The cyanide fishers profit by taking away from everyone else's trade and food. 'If people were using poison and my take dropped to only a little, I would accept it,' Puah said. "But I feel heartsick...I catch nothing at all. I have not caught a big fish in a month so there's no point in going fishing this afternoon". The local people are often helpless to protect themselves, as government and law enforcement officials have "open pockets" and are also involved in the trade by turning a blind eye to the illegal actions and receiving a take of the profits. "Culpability in cyanide use cannot be understood apart from the larger structures of corruption that permeates resource extraction throughout Indonesia. The Indonesian State bureaucracy extends from Jakarta down to the village level, and radiates out into villages through kinship connections. It is the factor most tightly correlated with illegal trade in natural resources throughout Indonesia".

Cause and Effect

Coral reefs found in the South Pacific are regarded as the "rainforest of the sea" harboring countless fish species large and small. However, recently the live fish trade has threatened the sanctity of these endangered areas. The Global Coral Reef Monitoring Network has issued a recent report that estimates that 25 per cent of the world's reefs are severely damaged and another third are in grave danger. The live fish trade is part of this alarming ecological trend caused by the popular use of cyanide which is injected into the coral reefs to stun inhabiting fish so they can be easily caught by nets. It is estimated that since the 1960s, more than one million kilograms of cyanide has been squirted into Philippine reefs alone, and since then the practice has spread throughout the South Pacific. The live fish trade is only growing, in 1994 the Philippines exported 200,000 kg of live fish; by 2004 the Philippines were annually exporting 800,000 kg annually. Although Asian markets are the primary buyers of live reef fish for food, the recently created U.S. Coral Reef Task Force has concluded that the U.S. is the primary purchaser of live reef fish for aquariums as well as eclectic jewelry. Even though the use of cyanide in the live fish trade is severely detrimental, one must realize that this issue is multidimensional. Small-scale native fishermen of the small South Pacific coastal communities are the backbone of the live fish trade, and are forced to resort to the illegal use of sodium cyanide due to demand and high prices offered by the industry.

Fishing Techniques

While live food fish trade can be very profitable for those involved, there are many dangerous aspects to it. Through the use of illegal practices such as cyanide fishing, coral reefs and fish communities are put in grave danger. The process of cyanide fishing involves injecting crushed cyanide tablets and squirting this solution from a bottle toward the targeted fish on top of coral heads. Specifically, the cyanide kills coral polyps, symbiotic algae, and other coral reefs organisms that are necessary for maintaining the health of the coral reef. These damages eventually deteriorate the coral reef and lead it into collapse of the entire coral reef ecosystem. The effect on the targeted fish is disorientation and semi-paralysis. After being squirted with cyanide the fish is easy brought to the surface and kept alive in small, on board container. Fishermen often understand that this practice is harmful and will offer locals a portion of the fish in order to continue fishing. When ingested, small levels of cyanide accumulate in the system causing weakness of fingers and toes, failure of the thyroid gland and blurred vision. Divers without experience may come in direct contact with cyanide, causing death. Estimates show that since the 1960's, over a million kilograms of cyanide have been squirted into the coral reefs of the Philippines alone. The harm upon the reefs is coming full circle and having a social impact through the limited fish stocks. As fish are depleted from these fishing techniques, the fishermen are having a more difficult time feeding themselves (Cyanide).

Additionally, the use of explosives may be used as a fishing technique in the live food fish trade. While the majority of these fish do not survive the blast of such explosions, the remaining fish that are only stunned are collected for the live food fish trade. The use of cyanide makes a stronger argument in that the more coral reef fish captured alive, the more lucrative the catch is for the fisherman. Live fish, according to the [WWF], fetch five times more than a dead fish (Cyanide). This is why banning the live-fish trade would similarly harm the reefs. Fisherman would resort to the "dead fish trade", be forced to deal in a larger quantity of fish, and the process of dangerous fishing techniques continues. To illustrate the effects of repeated explosions in the proximity of a coral reef system, roughly one half of the coral reefs in Komodo National Park in Indonesia have been destroyed. The use of cyanide and explosives in fishing proves to be an effective technique in catching fish, but its powers are indiscriminating and as a result the coral reefs are being held hostage to such practices. The future of the reefs are in question just as are the futures of those who subsist from them because "from a long term perspective, the question of ethics of using the ocean...contains a commitment for future generations".

In communities like those in the Philippines and Indonesia, people are participating in the live food fish trade because it is a source of income, or at least a source of temporary income. For some communities this is one of the few income-generating opportunities. Along with the environmental, ecological, and economic consequences of this industry, there are serious health risks as well. Because of inadequate training and lack of quality equipment, divers, especially young men are in large risk of paralysis.

Sustainable Practices

Because of the great profitability of this industry, there is a great incentive to identify sustainable practices. The

Marine Aquarium Council (MAC) works to offer the hobbyist with a product that is certified as environmentally sound and sustainable. Additionally, the International Marinelife Alliance (IMA), The Nature Conservancy (TNC), and MAC are working with the Hong Kong Chamber of Seafood Merchants to develop standards for the live fish trade. The Hong Kong Seafood Merchants represent ninety per cent of the buyers of live reef food fish in Hong Kong and have an extensive impact on collection practices.

In an effort to address the damage inflicted on coral reef eco-systems and fish stocks, aquaculture is being utilized to reduce pressure on coral reefs. However, initial efforts to farm grouper have met with significant challenges. There are difficulties with fragile grouper seed that can make it more expensive than wild caught larvae, which can affect natural replenishment rates. Additionally, there are problems with finding suitable food, disease and cannibalism. Efforts are also being made in regards to the aquarium fish trade. Juvenile fish are being captured and raised specifically for the industry. However, there are debates as to whether this practice will affect replenishment rates. "The age of the juveniles is pivotal to the debate, harvesting of postlarvae from the water column is considered to have a much lower (negligible) impact on rates of replenishment than the removal of the larger juveniles from benthic habitats because the postlarvae have yet to undergo severe mortality". If studies determine that the capture of juveniles is sustainable, it may help in mitigating the damage from cyanide fishing.

It should also be noted that aquaculture production, specifically grouper rearing is rapidly expanding in Asia. From 1998 to 2001 the Indo-Pacific countries involved in aquaculture; China, Indonesia, Republic of Korea, Kuwait, Malaysia, Philippines, Singapore, and Thailand witnessed a 119 per cent increase in output. The explosion in this practice can most likely be attributed to the large profit margins that can be derived in very little time. It is estimated that the majority of farms after annual returns can be paid back in less than one year. In comparison to other species of fish such as the Milkfish, the Grouper, because of high demand is able to garner high rates of return, in order to earn 1,000 dollars a grouper farm would only have to raise 400 kilograms in contrast to 5,000 kilograms of Milkfish.

CHAPTER

14

Fish Diseases and Parasites

Like humans and other animals, fish suffer from diseases and parasites. Fish defences against disease are specific and non-specific. Non-specific defences include skin and scales, as well as the mucus layer secreted by the epidermis that traps microorganisms and inhibits their growth. If pathogens breach these defences, fish can develop inflammatory responses that increase the flow of blood to infected areas and deliver white blood cells that attempt to destroy the pathogens.

Specific defences are specialised responses to particular pathogens recognised by the fish's body, that is immune responses. n recent years, vaccines have become widely used in aquaculture and ornamental fish, for example vaccines for furunculosis in farmed salmon and koi herpes virus in koi.

Some commercially important fish diseases are VHS, ich and whirling disease.

All fish carry pathogens and parasites. Usually this is at some cost to the fish. If the cost is sufficiently high, then the impacts can be characterised as a disease. However disease

From Top to Bottom: Pieces of the Carapace of *Litopenaeus vannamei*; a Harvested Healthy *L. vannamei* of size 66 (17 g); a dead *L. vannamei* infected by the Taura Syndrome Virus (TSV). The Colour of Healthy Shrimp is Determined by the Colour of the Plankton, the Type of Soil at the Pond Bottom, and the Additional Nutrients used. The White Color of the Shrimp at the Bottom is due to the TSV Infection

Oyster Reef At About Mid-tide Off Fishing Pier at Hunting Island State Park, South Carolina

Dulse is One of many Edible Algae

False-colour Scanning Electron Micrograph of the Unicellular Coccolithophore, *Gephyrocapsa oceanica*

Expressing Eggs from a Female Rainbow Trout

Shrimp Growout Pond on a Farm in South Korea

Tanks in a Shrimp Hatchery

A One-horsepower Paddlewheel Aerator.
The Splashing may Increase the Evaporation Rate of the Water
and thus Increase the Salinity of the Pond

Large Shrimp or Prawns for Sale in Italy

Harvesting of Kelp (*Saccharina latissima*, Previously Known As *Laminaria saccharina*) Cultivated in Proximity to Atlantic Salmon (*Salmo salar*) at Charlie Cove, Bay of Fundy, Canada

Macrobrachium Rosenbergii

Crustacea

Male Freshwater Phase Chinook

This Gizzard Shad has VHS, a Deadly Infectious Disease which Causes Bleeding. It Afflicts Over 50 Species of Freshwater and Marine Fish in the Northern Hemisphere

Cleaner Wrasses

A Shrimp Cocktail

The Plant Bed in An Aquaponic Systems

Salmon Farm in the Archipelago of Finland

Male Ocean Phase Chinook

Atlantic Salmon

Rainbow Trout

The Kelp Forest Exhibit at the Monterey Bay Aquarium.
A Three-dimensional, Multicellular Thallus

Koi (and Goldfish) have been Kept in Decorative Ponds for Centuries in China and Japan

A 3-tonne (3.0 LT; 3.3 ST) Great White Shark off Isla Guadalupe

A Small, Portable Aquaponics System

in fish is not understood well. What is known about fish disease often relates to aquaria fish, and more recently, to farmed fish.

Disease is a prime agent affecting fish mortality, especially when fish are young. Fish can limit the impacts of pathogens and parasites with behavioural or biochemical means, and such fish have reproductive advantages. Interacting factors result in low grade infection becoming fatal diseases. In particular, things that causes stress, such as natural droughts or pollution or predators, can precipitate outbreak of disease.

Disease can also be particularly problematic when pathogens and parasites carried by introduced species affect native species. An introduced species may find invading easier if potential predators and competitors have been decimated by disease.

Pathogens can cause fish diseases such as:

- viral disorders
- bacterial infections, such as *Pseudomonas fluorescens* leading to fin rot and fish dropsy
- fungal infections, such as saprolegnia
- mould infections, such as oomycete and saprolegnia

Parasites in fish are a natural occurrence and common. Parasites can provide information about host population ecology. In fisheries biology, for example, parasite communities can be used to distinguish distinct populations of the same fish species co-inhabiting a region. Additionally, parasites possess a variety of specialized traits and life-history strategies that enable them to colonize hosts. Understanding these aspects of parasite ecology, of interest in their own right, can illuminate parasite-avoidance strategies employed by hosts.

Usually parasites (and pathogens) need to avoid killing their hosts, since extinct hosts can mean extinct parasites. Evolutionary constraints may operate so parasites avoid killing their hosts, or the natural variability in host defensive strategies may suffice to keep host populations viable. Parasite infections can impair the courtship dance of male threespine sticklebacks. When that happens, the females reject them, suggesting a strong mechanism for the selection of parasite resistance."

However not all parasites want to keep their hosts alive, and there are parasites with multistage life cycles who go to some trouble to kill their host. For example, some tapeworms make some fish behave in such a way that a predatory bird can catch it. The predatory bird is the next host for the parasite in the next stage of its life cycle. Specifically, the tapeworm *Schistocephalus solidus* turns infected threespine stickleback white, and then makes them more buoyant so that they splash along at the surface of the water, becoming easy to see and easy to catch for a passing bird.

Other parasitic disorders, include *Gyrodactylus salaris, Ichthyophthirius multifiliis*, cryptocaryon, velvet disease, *Brooklynella hostilis*, Hole in the head, *Glugea, Ceratomyxa shasta, Kudoa thyrsites, Tetracapsuloides bryosalmonae, Cymothoa exigua*, leeches, nematode, flukes, *Platyhelminthes*, carp lice and salmon lice.

Some diseases result in mass die offs. One of the more bizarre and recently discovered diseases produces huge fish kills in shallow marine waters. It is caused by the ambush predator dinoflagellate *Pfiesteria piscicida*. When large numbers of fish, like shoaling forage fish, are in confined situations such as shallow bays, the excretions from the fish encourage this dinoflagellate, which is not normally toxic, to produce free-swimming zoospores. If the fish remain in the area, continuing to provide nourishment, then the zoospores start secreting a neurotoxin.

This toxin results in the fish developing bleeding lesions, and their skin flakes off in the water. The dinoflagellates then eat the blood and flakes of tissue while the affected fish die. Fish kills by this dinoflagellate are common, and they may also have been responsible for kills in the past which were thought to have had other causes. Kills like these can be viewed as natural mechanisms for regulating the population of exceptionally abundant fish. The rate at which the kills occur increases as organically polluted land runoff increases.

Some fish take advantage of cleaner fish for the removal of external parasites. The best known of these are the Bluestreak cleaner wrasses of the genus *Labroides* found on coral reefs in the Indian Ocean and Pacific Ocean. These small fish maintain so-called "cleaning stations" where other fish, known as hosts, will congregate and perform specific movements to attract the attention of the cleaner fish. Cleaning behaviours have been observed in a number of other fish groups, including an interesting case between two cichlids of the same genus, *Etroplus maculatus*, the cleaner fish, and the much larger *Etroplus suratensis*, the host.

More than 40 species of parasites may reside on the skin and internally of the ocean sunfish, motivating the fish to seek relief in a number of ways. In temperate regions, drifting kelp fields harbour cleaner wrasses and other fish which remove parasites from the skin of visiting sunfish. In the tropics, the *mola* will solicit cleaner help from reef fishes. By basking on its side at the surface, the sunfish also allows seabirds to feed on parasites from their skin. Sunfish have been reported to breach more than ten feet above the surface, possibly as another effort to dislodge parasites on the body.

According to Canadian biologist Dorothy Kieser, protozoan parasite *Henneguya salminicola* is commonly found in the flesh of salmonids. It has been recorded in the field samples of salmon returning to the Queen Charlotte Islands. The fish responds by walling off the parasitic infection into a number of cysts that contain milky fluid. This fluid is an accumulation of a large number of parasites.

Henneguya and other parasites in the myxosporean group have a complex lifecycle where the salmon is one of two hosts. The fish releases the spores after spawning. In the *Henneguya* case, the spores enter a second host, most likely an invertebrate, in the spawning stream. When juvenile salmon out-migrate to the Pacific Ocean, the second host releases a stage infective to salmon. The parasite is then carried in the salmon until the next spawning cycle. The myxosporean parasite that causes whirling disease in trout, has a similar lifecycle. However, as opposed to whirling disease, the *Henneguya* infestation does not appear to cause disease in the host salmon — even heavily infected fish tend to return to spawn successfully.

According to Dr. Kieser, a lot of work on *Henneguya salminicola* was done by scientists at the Pacific Biological Station in Nanaimo in the mid-1980s, in particular, an overview report which states that "the fish that have the longest fresh water residence time as juveniles have the most noticeable infections.

Hence in order of prevalence coho are most infected followed by sockeye, chinook, chum and pink." As well, the report says that, at the time the studies were conducted, stocks from the middle and upper reaches of large river systems in British Columbia such as Fraser, Skeena, Nass and from mainland coastal streams in the southern half of B.C. "are more likely to have a low prevalence of infection." The report also states "It should be stressed that *Henneguya*, economically deleterious though it is, is harmless from the view of public health. It is strictly a fish parasite that cannot live in or affect warm blooded animals, including man".

According to Klaus Schallie, Molluscan Shellfish Program Specialist with the Canadian Food Inspection Agency, "*Henneguya salminicola* is found in southern B.C. also and in all species of salmon. I have previously examined smoked chum salmon sides that were riddled with cysts and some sockeye runs in Barkley Sound (southern B.C., west coast of Vancouver Island) are noted for their high incidence of infestation."

Sea lice, particularly *Lepeophtheirus salmonis* and a variety of *Caligus* species, including *Caligus clemensi* and *Caligus rogercresseyi*, can cause deadly infestations of both farm-grown and wild salmon. Sea lice are ectoparasites which feed on mucous, blood, and skin, and migrate and latch onto the skin of wild salmon during free-swimming, planktonic *naupli* and *copepodid* larval stages, which can persist for several days.

Large numbers of highly populated, open-net salmon farms can create exceptionally large concentrations of sea lice; when exposed in river estuaries containing large numbers of open-net farms, many young wild salmon are infected, and do not survive as a result. Adult salmon may survive otherwise critical numbers of sea lice, but small, thin-skinned juvenile salmon migrating to sea are highly vulnerable. On the Pacific coast of Canada, the louse-induced mortality of pink salmon in some regions is commonly over 80 per cent.

In 1972, Gyrodactylus, a monogenean parasite, spread from Norwegian hatcheries to wild salmon, and devastated some wild salmon populations.

In 1984, infectious salmon anemia (ISAv) was discovered in Norway in an Atlantic salmon hatchery. Eighty per cent of the fish in the outbreak died. ISAv, a viral disease, is now a major threat to the viability of Atlantic salmon farming. It is now the first of the diseases classified on List One of the European Commission's Fish Health Regime. Amongst other measures, this requires the total eradication of the entire fish stock should an outbreak of the disease be confirmed on any farm. ISAv seriously affects salmon farms in Chile, Norway, Scotland and Canada, causing major economic losses to infected farms. As the name implies, it causes severe anemia of infected fish. Unlike mammals, the red blood cells of fish have DNA, and can become infected with viruses.

The fish develop pale gills, and may swim close to the water surface, gulping for air. However, the disease can also develop without the fish showing any external signs of illness, the fish maintain a normal appetite, and then they suddenly die. The disease can progress slowly throughout an infected farm and, in the worst cases, death rates may approach 100 per cent. It is also a threat to the dwindling stocks of wild salmon. Management strategies include developing a vaccine and improving genetic resistance to the disease.

In the wild, diseases and parasites are normally at low levels, and kept in check by natural predation on weakened individuals. In crowded net pens they can become epidemics. Diseases and parasites also transfer from farmed to wild salmon populations. A recent study in British Columbia links the spread of parasitic sea lice from river salmon farms to wild pink salmon in the same river." The European Commission concluded "The reduction of wild salmonid abundance is also linked to other factors but there is more and more scientific evidence establishing a direct link between the number of lice-infested wild fish and the presence of cages in the same estuary."

It is reported that wild salmon on the west coast of Canada are being driven to extinction by sea lice from nearby salmon farms. Antibiotics and pesticides are often used to control the diseases and parasites.

Ornamental fish kept in aquariums are susceptible to numerous diseases.

In most aquarium tanks, the fish are at high concentrations and the volume of water is limited. This means that communicable diseases can spread rapidly to most or all fish in a tank. An improper nitrogen cycle, inappropriate aquarium plants and potentially harmful freshwater invertebrates can directly harm or add to the stresses on ornamental fish in a tank. Despite this, many diseases in captive fish can be avoided or prevented through proper water conditions and a well-adjusted ecosystem within the tank. Ammonia poisoning is a common disease in new aquariums, especially when immediately stocked to full capacity.

Due to their generally small size and the low cost of replacing diseased or dead aquarium fish, the cost of testing and treating diseases is often seen as more trouble than the value of the fish.

The capture, transportation and culture of bait fish can spread damaging organisms between ecosystems, endangering them. Several American states, including Michigan, enacted regulations designed to slow the spread of fish diseases, including viral hemorrhagic septicemia, by bait fish. Because of the risk of transmitting *Myxobolus cerebralis* (whirling disease), trout and salmon should not be used as bait. Anglers may increase the possibility of contamination by emptying bait buckets into fishing venues and collecting or using bait improperly. The transportation of fish from one location to another can break the law and cause the introduction of fish and parasites alien to the ecosystem.

Though not a health concern in thoroughly cooked fish, parasites are a concern when human consumers eat raw or lightly preserved fish such as sashimi, sushi, ceviche, and gravlax. The popularity of such raw fish dishes makes it important for consumers to be aware of this risk. Raw fish should be frozen to an internal temperature of -20ºC (-4ºF) for at least 7 days to kill parasites. It is important to be aware that home freezers may not be cold enough to kill parasites.

Traditionally, fish that live all or part of their lives in fresh water were considered unsuitable for sashimi due to the possibility of parasites . Parasitic infections from freshwater fish are a serious problem in some parts of the world, particularly Southeast Asia. Fish that spend part of their life cycle in brackish or freshwater, like salmon are a particular problem. A study in Seattle, Washington showed that 100 per cent of wild salmon had roundworm larvae capable of infecting people. In the same study farm raised salmon did not have any roundworm larvae.

Parasite infection by raw fish is rare in the developed world (fewer than 40 cases per year in the U.S.), and involves mainly three kinds of parasites: Clonorchis sinensis (a trematode/fluke), Anisakis (a nematode/roundworm) and Diphyllobothrium (a cestode/tapeworm). Infection risk of anisakis is particularly higher in fishes which may live in a river such as salmon (*shake*) in Salmonidae, mackerel (*saba*). Such parasite infections can generally be avoided by boiling, burning, preserving in salt or vinegar, or freezing overnight. Even Japanese people never eat raw salmon and ikura, and even if they seem raw, these foods are not raw but are frozen overnight to prevent infections from parasites, particularly anisakis.

CHAPTER 15

Mariculture

Mariculture is a specialized branch of aquaculture involving the cultivation of marine organisms for food and other products in the open ocean, an enclosed section of the ocean, or in tanks, ponds or raceways which are filled with seawater. An example of the latter is the farming of marine fish, including finfish and shellfish e.g. prawns, or oysters and seaweed in saltwater ponds. Non-food products produced by mariculture include: fish meal, nutrient agar, jewellery (e.g. cultured pearls), and cosmetics.

Algae

Seawater algae such as kelp can be farmed in at least two ways. It can be grown around a rope that is anchored to the sea floor so that they do not drift away. Off the coast of California, boats with mowers harvest the top few feet of natural kelp beds. Kelp provides alginin, an edible material used in ice cream and cosmetics. The industry also supplies the dietary supplement industry.

Open Ocean

Raising marine organisms under controlled conditions in exposed, high-energy ocean environments beyond significant coastal influence,is a relatively new approach to mariculture. Open ocean aquaculture (OOA) Uses cages, nets, or long-line arrays that are moored, towed or float freely. Research and commercial open ocean aquaculture facilities are in operation or under development in Australia, Chile, China, France, Ireland, Italy, Japan, Mexico, and Norway. As of 2004, two commercial open ocean facilities were operating in U.S. waters, raising Threadfin near Hawaii and cobia near Puerto Rico. An operation targeting bigeye tuna recently received final approval. All U.S. commercial facilities are currently sited in waters under state or territorial jurisdiction.

Sea Ranching

The Japanese apply a principle based on behavioral conditioning and the migratory nature of certain species. The fishermen raise hatchlings in a closely knitted net in a harbor, sounding an underwater horn before each feeding. When the fish are old enough they are freed from the net to mature in the open sea. During spawning season, about 80 per cent of these fish return to their birthplace. The fishermen sound the horn and then net those fish that respond.

Seawater Ponds

In seawater pond mariculture, fish are raised in ponds which receive water from the sea. This has the benefit that the nutrition (e.g. microorganisms) present in the seawater can be used. This is a great advantage over traditional fish farms (e.g. sweet water farms) for which the farmers buy feed (which is expensive). Other advantages are that water purification plants may be planted in the ponds to eliminate the buildup of nitrogen, from fecal and other contamination. Also, the ponds can be left unprotected from natural predators, providing another kind of filtering.

Mariculture has rapidly expanded over the last two decades due to new technology, improvements in formulated feeds, greater biological understanding of farmed species, increased water quality within closed farm systems, greater demand for seafood products, site expansion and government interest . As a consequence, mariculture has been subject to some controversy regarding its social and environmental impacts . Commonly identified environmental impacts from marine farms are:

- Wastes from cage cultures;
- Farm escapees and invasives;
- Genetic pollution and disease and parasite transfer;
- Habitat modification.

As with most farming practices, the degree of environmental impact depends on the size of the farm, the cultured species, stock density, type of feed, hydrography of the site, and husbandry methods.

Mariculture of finfish can require a significant amount of fishmeal or other high protein food sources. Originally, a lot of fishmeal went to waste due to inefficient feeding regimes and poor digestibility of formulated feeds which resulted in poor feed conversion ratios.

In cage culture, several different methods are used for feeding farmed fish – from simple hand feeding to sophisticated computer-controlled systems with automated food dispensers coupled with *in situ* uptake sensors that detect consumption rates. In coastal fish farms, overfeeding primarily leads to increased disposition of detritus on the seafloor (potentially smothering seafloor dwelling invertebrates and altering the physical environment), while in hatcheries and land-based farms, excess food goes to waste and can potentially impact the surrounding catchment and local coastal environment This impact is usually highly local, and depends significantly on the settling velocity of waste feed and the current velocity (which varies both spatially and temporally) and depth.

Farm Escapees and Invasives

The impact of escapees from aquaculture operations depends on whether or not there are wild conspecifics or close relatives in the receiving environment, and whether or not the escapee is reproductively capable . Several different mitigation/prevention strategies are currently employed, from the development of infertile triploids to land-based farms which are completely isolated from any marine environment. Escapees can adversely impact local ecosystems through hybridization and loss of genetic diversity in native stocks, increase negative interactions within an ecosystem (such as predation and competition), disease transmission and habitat changes (from trophic cascades and ecosystem shifts to varying sediment regimes and thus turbidity).

The accidental introduction of invasive species is also of concern. Aquaculture is one of the main vectors for invasives following accidental releases of farmed stocks into the wild . One example is the Siberian sturgeon (*Acipenser baerii*) which accidentally escaped from a fish farm into the Gironde Estuary (Southwest France) following a severe storm in December 1999 (5,000 individual fish escaped into the estuary which had never hosted this species before). Molluscan farming is another example whereby species can be introduced to new environments by 'hitchhiking' on farmed molluscs. Also, farmed molluscs themselves can become dominate predators and/or competitors, as well as potentially spread pathogens and parasites.

Genetic Pollution and Disease and Parasite Transfer

One of the primary concerns with mariculture is the potential for disease and parasite transfer. Farmed stocks are often selectively bred to increase disease and parasite resistance, as well as improving growth rates and quality of products. As a consequence, the genetic diversity within reared stocks decreases with every generation - meaning they can potentially reduce the genetic diversity within wild populations if they escape into those wild populations. Such genetic pollution from escaped aquaculture stock can reduce the wild population's ability to adjust to the changing natural environment. Also, maricultured species can harbour diseases and parasites (e.g., lice) which can be introduced to wild populations upon their escape. An example of this is the parasitic sea lice on wild and farmed Atlantic salmon in Canada. Also, non-indigenous species which are farmed may have resistance to, or carry, particular diseases (which they picked up in their native habitats) which could be spread through wild populations if they escape into those wild populations. Such 'new' diseases would be devastating for those wild populations because they would have no immunity to them.

Habitat Modification

With the exception of benthic habitats directly beneath marine farms, most mariculture causes minimal destruction to habitats. However, the destruction of mangrove forests from the farming of shrimps is of concern. Globally, shrimp farming activity is a small contributor to the destruction of mangrove forests, however, locally it can be. devastating. Mangrove forests provide rich matrices which support a great deal of biodiversity – predominately juvenile fish and crustaceans. Furthermore, they act as buffering systems whereby they reduce coastal erosion, and improve water quality for in situ animals by processing material and 'filtering' sediments.

In addition, nitrogen and phosphorus compounds from food and waste may lead to blooms of phytoplankton, whose subsequent degradation can drastically reduce oxygen levels. If the algae are toxic, fish are killed and shellfish contaminated.

Sustainability

Mariculture development must be sustained by basic and applied research and development in major fields such as nutrition, genetics, system management, product handling, and socioeconomics. One approach is closed systems that have no direct interaction with the local environment. However, investment and operational cost are currently significantly higher than open cages, limiting them to their current role as hatcheries.

Potential Benefits

Sustainable mariculture promises economic and environmental benefits. Economies of scale imply that ranching can produce fish at lower cost than industrial fishing, leading to better human diets and the gradual elimination of unsustainable fisheries. Maricultured fish are also perceived to be of higher quality than fish raised in ponds or tanks, and offer more diverse choice of species. Consistent supply and quality control has enabled integration in food market channels.

Shellfish

Shellfish is a culinary and fisheries term for exoskeleton-bearing aquatic invertebrates used as food, including various species of molluscs, crustaceans, and echinoderms. Although most kinds of shellfish are harvested from saltwater environments, some kinds are found only in freshwater. In addition a few species of land crabs are eaten, for example *Cardisoma guanhumi* in the Caribbean.

The name "shellfish" is somewhat misleading, because shellfish are not related to fish in any way other than simply being animals. Many varieties of shellfish (crustaceans in particular) are actually closely related to insects and arachnids, making up one of the main classes of the phylum Arthropoda. Cephalopods (squid, octopus, cuttlefish) and bivalves (clams, oysters) are molluscs, as are snails and slugs.

Familiar marine molluscs enjoyed as a food source by humans include many species of clams, mussels, oysters, winkles, and scallops. Some crustaceans commonly eaten are shrimp, prawn, lobster, crayfish, and crabs. Echinoderms are not as frequently harvested for food as molluscs and crustaceans, however sea urchin roe is quite popular in many parts of the world.

Most shellfish eat a diet composed primarily of phytoplankton and zooplankton.

Shellfish are among the most common food allergens.

The term *shellfish* is used both broadly and specifically. In common parlance, as in having "shellfish" for dinner, it can refer to anything from clams and oysters to lobster and shrimp. For regulatory purposes it is often narrowly defined as *filter-feeding molluscs* such as clams, mussels, and oyster to the exclusion of crustaceans and all else.

Although the term is primarily applied to marine species, edible freshwater invertebrates such as crayfish and river mussels are also sometimes grouped under the umbrella of "shellfish".

Although their shells may differ, all shellfish are invertebrates. As non-mammalian animals that spend their entire lives in water they are "fish" in the logical sense; however the denotion *finfish* (or *finnicle fish*) has been developed to distinguish fish as animals *defined by having vertebrae* from shellfish in modern terminology.

The word "shellfish" is both singular and plural; the rarely used "shellfishes" is sometimes employed to distinguish among various types of shellfish.

Shellfish in Various Cuisines

Archaeological finds has shown that humans have been making use of shellfish as a food item for hundreds of thousands of years. In the present, shellfish dishes are a feature of almost all the cuisines of the world, providing an important source of protein in many cuisines around the world, especially in the countries with coastal areas.

In Japan

In the Japanese cuisine, chefs often use shellfish and their roe in different dishes. Sushi (vinegared rice, topped with other ingredients, including shellfish, fish, meat and vegetables), feature both raw and cooked shellfish. Sashimi primarily consists of very fresh raw seafood, sliced into thin pieces. Both sushi and sashimi are served with soy sauce and wasabi paste (a Japanese horseradish root, a spice with extremely strong hot flavor), thinly-sliced pickled ginger root, and a simple garnish such as shiso (a kitchen herb, member of the mint family) or finely shredded daikon radish, or both.

In the United States

Lobster in particular is a great delicacy in the United States, where families in the Northeast region make them into the centerpiece of a clam bake, usually for special occasions. Lobsters are eaten on much of the East Coast; the American lobster ranges from Newfoundland down to about the Carolinas, but is most often associated with Maine. A typical meal involves boiling the lobster with some slight seasoning and then serving it with drawn butter, baked potato, and corn on the cob.

Clamming is done both commercially and recreationally along the Northeast coastline of the US. Various type of clams are incorporated into the cuisine of New England. The soft-shelled clam is eaten either fried or steamed (and then called "steamers"). Many types of clams can be used for clam chowder, but the quahog, a hard shelled clam also known as a chowder clam, is often used because the long cooking time softens its tougher meat.

The Chesapeake Bay and Maryland region has generally been associated more with crabs, but in recent years the area has been trying to reduce its catch of blue crabs, as wild populations have been depleted. This has not, however, stemmed the demand: Maryland-style crabcakes are still a well known treat in crabhouses all over the bay, though the catch now comes from points farther south.

In the Southeast, and particularly the gulf states, shrimping is an important industry. Copious amounts of shrimp are harvested each year in the Gulf of Mexico and the Atlantic Ocean to satisfy a national demand for shrimp. Locally, prawns and shrimp are often deep fried; in the Cajun and Creole kitchens of Louisiana, shrimp and prawns are a common addition to traditional recipes like jambalaya and certain stews. Crayfish are a well known and much eaten delicacy here, often boiled in huge pots and heavily spiced.

In many major cities with active fishing ports, raw oyster bars are also a feature of shellfish consumption. When served freshly shucked (opened) and iced, one may find a liquid inside the shell, called the liqueur. Some believe that oysters have the properties of an aphrodisiac.

Inter-tidal herbivorous shellfish such as mussels and clams can help people reach a healthy balance of omega-3 and omega-6 fats in their diets, instead of the current Western diets. For this reason, the eating of shellfish is often encouraged by dietitians.

Jewish Kosher Law traditions forbid the eating of shellfish. The book of Leviticus prohibits the consumption of shellfish. In Islam, one Sunni school of thought (*Hanafi*) forbids eating shellfish, while the other three Sunni schools allow it. The Shi'ite school (*Ja'fari*) does not allow it. Seventh-day Adventists believe that they should not eat shellfish. Rastafarians as well do not eat shellfish.

CHAPTER

16

Integrated Multi-tropic Aquaculture

Integrated Multi-Trophic Aquaculture (IMTA) provides the by-products, including waste, from one aquatic species as inputs (fertilizers, food) for another. Farmers combine fed aquaculture (e.g., fish, shrimp) with inorganic extractive (e.g., seaweed) and organic extractive (e.g., shellfish) aquaculture to create balanced systems for environment remediation (biomitigation), economic stability (improved output, lower cost, product diversification and risk reduction) and social acceptability (better management practices).

Selecting appropriate species and sizing the various populations to provide necessary ecosystem functions allows the biological and chemical processes involved to achieve a stable balance, mutually benefiting the organisms and improving ecosystem health.

Ideally, the co-cultured species each yield valuable commercial "crops". IMTA can synergistically increase total output, even if some of the crops yield less than they would, short-term, in a monoculture.

"Integrated" refers to intensive and synergistic cultivation, using water-born nutrient and energy transfer. "Multi-trophic" means that the various species occupy different trophic levels, i.e., different (but adjacent) links in the food chain.

IMTA is a specialized form of the age-old practice of aquatic polyculture, which was the co-culture of various species, often without regard to trophic level. In this broader case, the organisms may share biological and chemical processes that are minimally complementary, potentially leading to significant ecosystem shifts/damage. Some traditional systems did culture species that occupied multiple niches within the same pond, but with limited intensity and management.

The more general term "Integrated Aquaculture" is used to describe the integration of monocultures through water transfer. The terms "IMTA" and "integrated aquaculture" differ primarily in their precision and are sometimes interchanged. Aquaponics, fractionated aquaculture, IAAS (integrated agriculture-aquaculture systems), IPUAS (integrated peri-urban-aquaculture systems), and IFAS (integrated fisheries-aquaculture systems) are variations on the IMTA concept.

Today, low intensity traditional/incidental multi-trophic aquaculture is much more common than modern IMTA. Most are relatively simple, such as fish/seaweed/shellfish.

True IMTA can be land-based, using ponds or tanks, or open-water marine or freshwater systems. Implementations have included species combinations such as shellfish/shrimp, fish/seaweed/shellfish, fish/shrimp and seaweed/shrimp.

In the future, systems with other components for additional functions, or similar functions but different size brackets of particles, are likely. Multiple regulatory issues remain open.

Modern History of Land-based Systems

Ryther and co-workers created modern, integrated, intensive, land mariculture. They originated, both theoretically and experimentally, the integrated use of extractive organisms—shellfish, microalgae and seaweeds—in the treatment of household effluents, descriptively and with quantitative results.

A domestic wastewater effluent, mixed with seawater, was the nutrient source for phytoplankton, which in turn became food for oysters and clams. They cultivated other organisms in a food chain rooted in the farm's organic sludge. Dissolved nutrients in the final effluent were filtered by seaweed (mainly Gracilaria and Ulva) biofilters. The value of the original organisms grown on human waste effluents was minimal.

In 1976, Huguenin proposed adaptations to the treatment of intensive aquaculture effluents in both inland and coastal areas. Tenore followed by integrating with their system of carnivorous fish and the macroalgivore abalone.

In 1977, Hughes-Games described the first practical marine fish/shellfish/phytoplankton culture, followed by Gordin, *et al.*, in 1981. By 1989, a semi-intensive (1 kg fish/m^{-3}) seabream and grey mullet pond system by the Gulf of Aqaba (Eilat) on the Red Sea supported dense diatom populations, excellent for feeding oysters. Hundreds of kilos of fish and oysters cultured here were sold. Researchers also quantified the water quality parameters and nutrient budgets in (5 kg fish m^{-3}) green water seabream ponds.

The phytoplankton generally maintained reasonable water quality and converted on average over half the waste nitrogen into algal biomass. Experiments with intensive bivalve cultures yielded high bivalve growth rates. This technology supported a small farm in southern Israel.

IMTA promotes economic and environmental sustainability by converting byproducts and uneaten feed from fed organisms into harvestable crops, thereby reducing eutrophication, and increasing economic diversification.

Properly managed multi-trophic aquaculture accelerates growth without detrimental side-effects. This increases the site's ability to assimilate the cultivated organisms, thereby reducing negative environmental impacts.

IMTA enables farmers to diversify their output by replacing purchased inputs with byproducts from lower trophic levels, often without new sites. Initial economic research suggests that IMTA can increase profits and can reduce financial risks due to weather, disease and market fluctuations. Over a dozen studies have investigated the economics of IMTA systems since 1985.

Nutrient Flow

Typically, carnivorous fish or shrimp occupy IMTA's higher trophic levels. They excrete soluble ammonia and phosphorus (orthophosphate). Seaweeds and similar species can extract these inorganic nutrients directly from their environment. Fish and shrimp also release organic nutrients which feed shellfish and deposit feeders.

Species such as shellfish that occupy intermediate trophic levels often play a dual role, both filtering organic bottom-level organisms from the water and generating some ammonia. Waste feed may also provide additional nutrients; either by direct consumption or via decomposition into individual nutrients.

Recovery Efficiency

Nutrient recovery efficiency is a function of technology, harvest schedule, management, spatial configuration, production, species selection, trophic level biomass ratios, natural food availability, particle size, digestibility, season, light, temperature, and water flow. Since these factors significantly vary by site and region, recovery efficiency also varies.

In a hypothetical family-scale fish/microalga /bivalve/ seaweed farm, based on pilot scale data, at least 60 per cent of nutrient input reached commercial products, nearly three times more than in modern net pen farms. Expected average annual yields of the system for a hypothetical 1 hectare (2.5 acres) were 35 tonnes (34 LT; 39 ST) of seabream, 100 tonnes (98 LT; 110 ST) of bivalves and 125 tonnes (123 LT; 138 ST) of seaweeds. These results required precise water quality control and attention to suitability for bivalve nutrition, due to the difficulty in maintaining consistent phytoplanton populations.

Seaweeds' nitrogen uptake efficiency ranges from 2-100 per cent in land-based systems. Uptake efficiency in open-water IMTA is unknown.

Food Safety and Quality

Feeding the wastes of one species to another has the potential for contamination, although this has yet to be observed in IMTA systems. Mussels and kelp growing adjacent to Atlantic salmon cages in the Bay of Fundy have been monitored since 2001 for contamination by medicines, heavy metals, arsenic, PCBs and pesticides. Concentrations are consistently either non-detectable or well below regulatory limits established by the Canadian Food Inspection Agency, the United States Food and Drug Administration and European Community Directives.

Taste testers indicate that these mussels are free of "fishy" taste and aroma and could not distinguish them from "wild" mussels. The mussels' meat yield is significantly higher, reflecting the increase in nutrient availability.

Asia

Japan, China, South Korea, Thailand, Vietnam, Indonesia, etc. have co-cultured aquatic species for centuries in marine, brackish and fresh water environments. Fish, shellfish and seaweeds have been cultured together in bays, lagoons and ponds. Trial and error has improved integration over time. The proportion of Asian aquaculture production that occurs in IMTA systems is unknown.

Canada

Bay of Fundy

Industry, academia and government are collaborating here to expand production to commercial scale. The current system integrates Atlantic salmon, blue mussels and kelp; deposit feeders are under consideration. AquaNet (one of Canada's Networks of Centers of Excellence) funded phase one. The Atlantic Canada Opportunities Agency is presently funding phase two. The project leaders are Thierry Chopin (University of New Brunswick in Saint John) and Shawn Robinson (Department of Fisheries and Oceans, St. Andrews Biological Station).

Pacific SEA-lab

Pacific SEA-lab is researching and is licensed for the co-culture of sablefish, scallops, oysters, blue mussels, urchins and kelp. "SEA" stands for Sustainable Ecological Aquaculture. The project presently aims to balance four species.The project is headed by Stephen Cross under a British Columbia Innovation Award at the University of Victoria Coastal Aquaculture Research & Training (CART) network.

Chile

The i-mar Research Center at the Universidad de Los Lagos, in Puerto Montt is working to reduce the environmental impact of intensive salmon culture. Initial research involved trout, oysters and seaweeds. Present research is focusing on open waters with salmon, seaweeds and abalone. The project leader is Alejandro Buschmann.

Israel

Sea or Marine Enterprises Ltd.

Sea or Marine Enterprises Ltd., which operated for several years on the Israeli Mediterranean coast, north of Tel Aviv, cultured marine fish (gilthead seabream), seaweeds (Ulva and Gracilaria) and Japanese abalone. Its approach leveraged local climate, and recycled fish waste products into seaweed biomass, which was fed to the abalone. It also effectively purified the water sufficiently to allow the water to be recycled to the fishponds and to meet point-source effluent environmental regulations.

PGP Ltd.

PGP Ltd. is a small farm in Southern Israel. It cultures marine fish, microalgae, bivalves and Artemia. Effluents from seabream and seabass collect in sedimentation ponds, where dense populations of microalgae—mostly diatoms—develop. Clams, oysters and sometimes Artemia filter the microalgae from the water, producing a clear effluent. The farm sells the fish, bivalves and Artemia.

South Africa

Three farms currently grow seaweeds for feed in abalone effluents in land-based tanks. Up to 50 per cent of re-circulated water passes through the seaweed tanks. Somewhat uniquely, neither fish nor shrimp comprise the upper trophic species. The motivation is to avoid over-harvesting natural seaweed beds and red tides, rather than nutrient abatement. These commercial successes developed from research collaboration between Irvine and Johnson Cape Abalone and scientists from the University of Cape Town and the University of Stockholm.

United Kingdom

The Scottish Association for Marine Science, in Oban is developing co-cultures of salmon, oysters, sea urchins, and brown and red seaweeds via several projects. Research focuses on biological and physical processes, as well as production economics and implications for coastal zone management. Researchers include: M. Kelly, A. Rodger, L. Cook, S. Dworjanyn, and C. Sanderson.

Other Projects

Several other projects over the last three decades have aided IMTA development.

CHAPTER

17

Freshwater Prawn Farm

A freshwater prawn farm is an aquaculture business designed to raise and produce freshwater prawn or shrimp1 for human consumption. Freshwater prawn farming shares many characteristics with, and many of the same problems as, marine shrimp farming. Unique problems are introduced by the developmental life cycle of the main species (the giant river prawn, *Macrobrachium rosenbergii*).

The global annual production of freshwater prawns (excluding crayfish and crabs) in 2003 was about 280,000 tons, of which China produced some 180,000 tons, followed by India and Thailand with some 35,000 tons each. Additionally, China produced about 370,000 tons of Chinese river crab (*Eriocheir sinensis*).

All farmed freshwater prawns today belong to the genus *Macrobrachium*. Until 2000, the only species farmed was the Giant river prawn (*Macrobrachium rosenbergii*, also known as the Malaysian prawn). Since then, China has begun farming the Oriental river prawn (*M. nipponense*) in large quantities, and India farms a small amount of monsoon river prawn

(*M. malcolmsonii*). In 2003, these three species accounted for all farmed freshwater prawns, about two thirds *M. rosenbergii* and one third *M. nipponense*.

There are about 200 species in the genus *Macrobrachium*. They occur throughout the tropics and subtropics on all continents except Europe.

Giant river prawns live in turbid freshwater, but their larval stages require brackish water to survive. Males can reach a body size of 32 cm;females grow to 25 cm. In mating, the male deposits spermatophores on the underside of the female's thorax, between the walking legs. The female then extrudes eggs, which pass through the spermatophores. The female carries the fertilized eggs with her until they hatch; the time may vary, but is generally less than three weeks. A large female may lay up to 100,000 eggs.

From these eggs hatch zoeae, the first larval stage of crustaceans. They go through several larval stages before metamorphosing into postlarvae, at which stage they are about 8 mm long and have all the characteristics of adults. This metamorphosis usually takes place about 32 to 35 days after hatching. These postlarvae then migrate back into freshwater.

There are three different morphotypes of males. The first stage is called "small male" (SM); this smallest stage has short, nearly translucent claws. If conditions allow, small males grow and metamorphose into "orange claws" (OC), which have large orange claws on their second chelipeds, which may have a length of 0.8 to 1.4 their body size. OC males later may transform into the third and final stage, the "blue claw" (BC) males. These have blue claws, and their second chelipeds may become twice as long as their body.

Male *M. rosenbergii* have a strict hierarchy: the territorial BC males dominate the OCs, which in turn dominate the SMs. The presence of BC males inhibts the growth of SMs and delays the metamorphosis of OCs into BCs; an OC will keep growing until it is larger than the largest BC male in its neighbourhood before transforming. All three male stages are sexually active though, and females who have undergone their pre-mating molt will cooperate with any male to reproduce. BC males protect the female until their shell has hardened, OCs and SMs show no such behaviour.

Giant River Prawns have been farmed using traditional methods in south-east Asia for a long time. First experiments with artificial breeding cultures of *M. rosenbergii* were done in the early 1960s in Malaysia, where it was discovered that the larvae needed brackish water for survival. Industrial-scale rearing processes were perfected in the early 1970s in Hawaii, and spread then first to Taiwan and Thailand and then to other countries.

The technologies used in freshwater prawn farming are basically the same as in marine shrimp farming. hatcheries produce postlarvae, which then are grown and acclimated in nurseries before being transferred into growout ponds, where the prawns are then fed and grown until they reach marketable size. Harvesting is done by either draining the pond and collecting the animals ("batch" harvesting) or by fishing the prawns out of the pond using nets (continuous operation).

Due to the aggressive nature of *M. rosenbergii* and the hierarchy between males, stocking densities are much lower than in penaeid shrimp farms. Intensive farming is not possible due to the increased level of cannibalism, so all farms are either stocked semi-intensively (4 to 20 postlarvae per square metre) or, in extensive farms, at even lower densities (1 to 4/ m^2). The management of the growout ponds must take into account the growth characteristics of *M. rosenbergii*: the presence of blue-claw males inhibits the growth of small males, and delays the metamorphosis of OC males into blue-claws. Some farms fish off the largest prawns from the pond using seines to ensure a healthy composition of the pond's population, designed to optimize the yield, even if they employ batch harvesting. The heterogeneous individual growth of *M. rosenbergii* makes growth control necessary even if a pond is stocked newly, starting from scratch: some animals will grow faster than others and become dominant BCs, shunting the growth of other individuals.

The FAO considers the ecological impact of freshwater prawn farming to be less severe than in shrimp farming. The prawns are cultured at much lower densities, meaning less concentrated waste products and a lesser danger of the ponds becoming breeding places for diseases. The growout ponds do not salinate agricultural land, as do those of inland marine shrimp farms. Freshwater prawn farms do not endanger mangroves, and are better amenable to small-scale businesses run by a family. However, like marine farmed shrimp, *M. rosenbergii* is also susceptible to a variety of viral or bacterial diseases, including the White Tail Disease , also called "White Muscle Disease".

The global annual production of freshwater prawns in 2003 was about 280,000 tonnes, of which China produced some 180,000 tonnes, followed by India and Thailand with some 35,000 tonnes each. Other major producer countries are Taiwan, Bangladesh, and Vietnam. In the United States, there are only a few hundred small farms for *M. rosenbergii* with an overall production of just about 50 tonnes in 2003. The U.S. is, though, the largest producer of farmed crayfish. In 2003, U.S. farms produced 33,500 tonnes of red swamp crawfish (*Procambarus clarkii*), a crayfish species native to North America.

Macrobrachium Rosenbergii

Macrobrachium rosenbergii, also known as the giant river prawn, the giant freshwater prawn, the Malaysian prawn, freshwater scampi (especially in India), or the cherabin, is a species of freshwater shrimp (not a prawn or scampo in terms of phylogeny, although colloquially "prawn" can refer to freshwater shrimp or true prawns) native to the Indo-Pacific and northern Australia. This species (as well as other *Macrobrachium*) is commercially important for its value as a food source.

While this species is considered a freshwater one, the larval stage of the animal depends on brackish water. Once the individual shrimp has grown beyond the planktonic stage and become a juvenile, it will live entirely in freshwater.

This species of shrimp can get quite large, attaining a length of over 30 cm (12 inches).

Males can reach a body size of 32 cm;females grow to 25 cm. In mating, the male deposits spermatophores on the underside of the female's thorax, between the walking legs. The female then extrudes eggs, which pass through the spermatophores. The female carries the fertilized eggs with her until they hatch; the time may vary, but is generally less than three weeks. A large female may lay up to 100,000 eggs.

The shrimp can be successfully raised in outdoor ponds and is readily available for sale on the Internet. Amateur cultivation of this species is particularly popular in the Midwestern region of the United States.

Crustacean

Crustaceans (Crustacea) form a very large group of arthropods, usually treated as a subphylum, which includes such familiar animals as crabs, lobsters, crayfish, shrimp, krill and barnacles. The 50,000 described species range in size from *Stygotantulus stocki* at 0.1 mm (0.004 in), to the Japanese spider crab with a leg span of up to 12.5 ft (3.8 m) and a mass of 44 lb (20 kg). Like other arthropods, crustaceans have an exoskeleton, which they moult to grow. They are distinguished from other groups of arthropods, such as insects, myriapods and chelicerates by the possession of biramous (two-parted) limbs, and by the nauplius form of the larvae.

Most crustaceans are free-living aquatic animals, but some are terrestrial (e.g. woodlice), some are parasitic (e.g. fish lice, tongue worms) and some are sessile (e.g. barnacles). The group has an extensive fossil record, reaching back to the Cambrian, and includes living fossils such as *Triops cancriformis*, which has existed apparently unchanged since the Triassic period. More than 10 million tons of crustaceans are produced by fishery or farming for human consumption, the majority of it being shrimps and prawns. Krill and copepods are not as widely fished, but may be the animals with the greatest biomass on the planet, and form a vital part of the food chain. The scientific study of crustaceans is known as carcinology (alternatively, malacostracology, crustaceology or crustalogy), and a scientist who works in carcinology is a carcinologist.

The body of a crustacean is composed of body segments, which are grouped into three regions: the *cephalon* or head, the thorax, and the *pleon* or abdomen. The head and thorax may be fused together to form a cephalothorax, which may be covered by a single large carapace. The crustacean body is protected by the hard exoskeleton, which must be moulted for the animal to grow. The shell around each somite can be divided into a dorsal tergum, ventral sternum and a lateral pleuron. Various parts of the exoskeleton may be fused together.

Each somite, or body segment can bear a pair of appendages: on the segments of the head, these include two pairs of antennae, the mandibles and maxillae; the thoracic segments bear legs, which may be specialised as pereiopods (walking legs) and maxillipeds (feeding legs). The abdomen bears pleopods, and ends in a telson, which bears the anus, and is often flanked by uropods to form a tail fan. The number and variety of appendages in different crustaceans may be partly responsible for the group's success. Crustacean appendages are typically biramous, meaning they are divided into two parts; this includes the second pair of antennae, but not the first, which is uniramous. It is unclear whether the biramous condition is a derived state which evolved in crustaceans, or whether the second branch of the limb has been lost in all other groups. Trilobites, for instance, also possessed biramous appendages.

The main body cavity is an open circulatory system, where blood is pumped into the haemocoel by a heart located near the dorsum. The alimentary canal consists of a straight tube that often has a gizzard-like "gastric mill" for grinding food and a pair of digestive glands that absorb food; this structure goes in a spiral format. Structures that function as kidneys are located near the antennae. A brain exists in the form of ganglia close to the antennae, and a collection of major ganglia is found below the gut.

In many decapods, the first (and sometimes the second) pair of pleopods are specialised in the male for sperm transfer. Many terrestrial crustaceans (such as the Christmas Island red crab) mate seasonally and return to the sea to release the eggs. Others, such as woodlice, lay their eggs on land, albeit in damp conditions. In most decapods, the females retain the eggs until they hatch into free-swimming larvae.

Ecology

The majority of crustaceans are aquatic, living in either marine or fresh water environments, but a few groups have adapted to life on land, such as terrestrial crabs, terrestrial hermit crabs, and woodlice. Marine crustaceans are as ubiquitous in the oceans as insects are on land. The majority of crustaceans are also motile, moving about independently, although a few taxonomic units are parasitic and live attached to their hosts (including sea lice, fish lice, whale lice, tongue worms, and *Cymothoa exigua*, all of which may be referred to as "crustacean lice"), and adult barnacles live a sessile life – they are attached headfirst to the substrate and cannot move independently. Some branchiurans are able to withstand rapid changes of salinity and will also switch hosts from marine to non-marine species. Krill are the bottom layer and the most important part of the food chain in Antarctic animal communities. Some crustaceans are significant invasive species, such as the Chinese mitten crab and the Asian shore crab.

LIFE CYCLE

Mating System

The majority of crustaceans have separate sexes, and reproduce sexually. A small number are hermaphrodites, including barnacles, remipedes, and Cephalocarida. Some may even change sex during the course of their life. Parthenogenesis is also widespread among crustaceans, where viable eggs are produced by a female without needing fertilisation by a male. This occurs in many brachiopods, some ostracods, some isopods, and certain "higher" crustaceans, such as the *Marmorkrebs* crayfish.

Eggs

In many groups of crustaceans, the fertilised eggs are simply released into the water column, while others have developed a number of mechanisms for holding on to the eggs until they are ready to hatch. Most decapods carry the eggs attached to the pleopods, while peracarids, notostracans, anostracans, and many isopods form a brood pouch from the carapace and thoracic limbs. Female Branchiura do not carry eggs in external ovisacs but attach them in rows to rocks and other objects. Most leptostracans and krill carry the eggs between their thoracic limbs; some copepods carry their eggs in special thin-walled sacs, while others have them attached together in long, tangled strings.

Larvae

Crustaceans exhibit a number of larval forms, of which the earliest and most characteristic is the nauplius. This has three pairs of appendages, all emerging from the young animal's head, and a single naupliar eye. In most groups, there are further larval stages, including the zoea . This name was given to it when naturalists believed it to be a separate species. It follows the nauplius stage and precedes the post-larva. Zoea larvae swim with their thoracic appendages, as opposed to nauplii, which use cephalic appendages, and megalopa, which use abdominal appendages for swimming. It often has spikes on its carapace, which may assist these small organisms in maintaining directional swimming. In many decapods, due to their accelerated development, the zoea is the first larval stage. In some cases, the zoea stage is followed by the mysis stage, and in others, by the megalopa stage, depending on the crustacean group involved.

Classification

The name "crustacean" dates from the earliest works to describe the animals, including those of Pierre Belon and Guillaume Rondelet, but the name was not used by some later authors, including Carl Linnaeus, who included crustaceans among the "Aptera" in his *Systema Naturae*. The earliest nomenclaturally valid work to use the name "Crustacea" was Morten Thrane Brünnich's *Zoologiæ Fundamenta* in 1772, although he also included chelicerates in the group.

The subphylum Crustacea comprises almost 52,000 described species, although the number of undescribed species may be 10-100 times higher. Although most crustaceans are small, their morphology varies greatly and they include both the largest arthropod in the world – the Japanese spider crab with a leg span of 14 feet (4.3 m) – and the smallest – the 0.1 mm (0.004 in) long *Stygotantulus stocki*. Despite their diversity of form, crustaceans are united by the special larval form known as the nauplius.

The exact relationships of the Crustacea to other taxa are not yet entirely clear. Under the Pancrustacea hypothesis, Crustacea and Hexapoda (insects and allies) are sister groups. Studies using DNA sequences tend to show a paraphyletic Crustacea, with the insects (but not necessarily other hexapods) nested within that clade. Although the classification of crustaceans has been quite variable, the system used by Martin and Davis is the most authoritative, and largely supersedes earlier works. Mystacocarida and Branchiura, here treated as part of Maxillopoda, are sometimes treated as their own classes.

Crustaceans have a rich and extensive fossil record, which begins with animals such as *Canadaspis* and *Perspicaris* from the Middle Cambrian age Burgess Shale. Most of the major groups of crustaceans appear in the fossil record before the end of the Cambrian, namely the Branchiopoda, Maxillopoda (including barnacles and tongue worms) and Malacostraca; there is some debate as to whether or not Cambrian animals assigned to Ostracoda are truly ostracods, which would otherwise start in the Ordovician. The only classes to appear later are the Cephalocarida, which have no fossil record, and the Remipedia, which were first described from the fossil *Tesnusocaris goldichi*, but do not appear until the Carboniferous.

Most of the early crustaceans are rare, but fossil crustaceans become abundant from the Carboniferous onwards.

Within the Malacostraca, no fossils are known for krill, while both Hoplocarida and Phyllopoda contain important groups that are now extinct as well as extant members (Hoplocarida: mantis shrimp are extant, while Aeschronectida are extinct; Phyllopoda: Canadaspidida are extinct, while Leptostraca are extant). Cumacea and Isopoda are both known from the Carboniferous, as are the first true mantis shrimp. In the Decapoda, prawns and polychelids appear in the Triassic, and shrimp and crabs appear in the Jurassic; however, the great radiation of crustaceans occurred in the Cretaceous, particularly in crabs, and may have been driven by the adaptive radiation of their main predators, bony fish. The first true lobsters also appear in the Cretaceous.

Many crustaceans are consumed by humans, and nearly 10,700,000 tons were produced in 2007; the vast majority of this output is of decapod crustaceans: crabs, lobsters, shrimp, and prawns. Over 60 per cent by weight of all crustaceans caught for consumption are shrimp and prawns, and nearly 80 per cent is produced in Asia, with China alone producing nearly half the world's total. Non-decapod crustaceans are not widely consumed, with only 118,000 tons of krill being caught, despite krill having one of the greatest biomasses on the planet.

Bibliography

Corpron, K.E., Armstrong, D.A., 1983. Removal of Nitrogen by An Aquatic Plant, *Elodea densa*, in Recirculating *Macrobrachium* Culture Systems. *Aquaculture* 32, 347-360.

Duarte, Carlos M; Marbá, Nùria and Holmer, Marianne (2007) *Rapid Domestication of Marine Species*. Science. Vol. 316, No. 5823, pp. 382-383.

J.G. Ferreira, A.J.S. Hawkins, S.B. Bricker, 2007. Management of Productivity, Environmental Effects and Profitability of Shellfish Aquaculture — The Farm Aquaculture Resource Management (FARM) Model. *Aquaculture*, 264, 160-174.

GESAMP (2008) *Assessment and Communication of Environmental Risks in Coastal Aquaculture* FAO Reports and Studies No. 76.

Hepburn, J. 2002. *Taking Aquaculture Seriously*. Organic Farming, Winter 2002, Soil Association.

Kinsey, Darin, 2006 "Seeding the Water as the Earth": Epicentre and Peripheries of a Global Aquacultural Revolution. *Environmental History* 11, 3: 527-66.

Naylor, R.L., S.L. Williams, and D.R. Strong. 2001. *Aquaculture* – A Gateway for Exotic Species. Science, 294: 1655-6.

The Scottish Association for Marine Science and Napier University. 2002. *Review and Synthesis of the Environmental Impacts of Aquaculture*.

Higginbotham James *Piscinae: Artificial Fishponds in Roman Italy* University of North Carolina Press (June, 1997).

Wyban, Carol Araki (1992) *Tide and Current: Fishponds of Hawai'I* University of Hawaii Press: ISBN 0-8248-1396-0.

Timmons, M.B., Ebeling, J.M., Wheaton, F.W., Summerfelt, S.T., Vinci, B.J., 2002. Recirculating Aquaculture Systems: 2nd Edition. Cayuga Aqua Ventures.

Piedrahita, R.H., 2003. Reducing the Potential Environmental Impacts of Tank Aquaculture Effluents Through Intensification and Recirculation. *Aquaculture* 226, 35-44.

Klas, S., Mozes, N., Lahav, O., 2006. Development of a Single-sludge Denitrification Method for Nitrate Removal from RAS Effluents: Lab-scale Results vs. Model Prediction. *Aquaculture* 259, 342-353.

Index

N

O

P

R

S

T